C000130857

PUFFER AHOY!

PUFFER AHOY!

BY

GEORGE W. BURROWS

GLASGOW
BROWN, SON & FERGUSON LTD., NAUTICAL PUBLISHERS
52 DARNLEY STREET

Copyright in all Countries signatory to the Berne Convention
All rights reserved

First Edition   *1981*

ISBN 0 85174 419 2

© 1981—BROWN, SON & FERGUSON, LTD., GLASGOW G41 2SG

FOREWORD

THE 'Clyde Puffer' was so called at its inception around the 1850s. Its propelling unit consisted of a single-cylinder engine without a condenser: the steam from the cylinder simply exhausted to the atmosphere and was lost. The action of the single-cylinder engine was, as the name implies, a persistent 'puff-puff' up through the funnel, with a resultant heavy wastage of fuel. By about 1870 this type of craft was extensively used in canal work. Later vessels of this type were equipped with condensing compound power units. In these the engine comprised a high-pressure and a low-pressure cylinder, the steam passing from one to the other, and thereafter through the condenser, re-entering the boiler via the feed-pump. This completed the cycle, and a much wider scope became available to these sturdy boats. They were no longer confined to canal work, but were now able to venture to open sea-water, which made it possible to load cargoes for the Western Isles, and even Ireland, with fresh boiler water no longer a problem. The transformation meant that, in effect, they no longer were literally 'Puffers', although the description persisted, and still remains, even for their Diesel-engined successors.

The modern, privately-owned Puffer, such as the *Petrel*, was almost yacht-like in appearance. The deck was painted a buff colour and, on one occasion, with a cargo of coal, with the usual hosing down and the black funnel and copper waste-pipe cleaned and burnished, she was a picture when proceeding on a flood-tide. It was known with the cleavage of water at the bow that 'she had a good bone in her teeth'. It was not unknown to slacken back the boiler safety-valve enough to give the impression of speed, thus producing 'steam at the waste-pipe', and the impression of a good head of steam. This was occasionally done on meeting another Puffer.

The shipyard of Maryhill, latterly known as Kelvindock, built some 70 Puffers between 1865 and 1920, the last iron-built vessel being the *Sterlina*, latterly owned by Richard Burrows.

The last two then modern Puffers were completed in 1920, namely the *Kype* and the *Logan*—built to the order of Dickson & Co. The former is seen being launched broadside in 1920. They carried approximately 120 tons.

Some Puffers, built at Kelvindock for Paton & Hendry, were fitted with tandem compound engines. The one cylinder was assembled on top of the other, with a common piston rod; and the arrangement was quite successful. An example was found on the *Gnome*, which made some comparatively fast runs.

Alcohol, one feels, frequently played its nefarious part in the operation (or lack of it) of these vessels, with cost to human lives. One feels that too many of these craft were operated in a haphazard manner—in particular, journeys made unhatched resulted in sinking and loss of life.

The evolution of the Puffer shows what a change this craft has experienced. To begin with, it had very little character. A single cylinder with complete discharge to the atmosphere; either a steering-wheel or a long tiller, one or the other entirely exposing to the weather a man standing on a duckboard. It was not until the early 1920s that an attempt was made to protect the helmsman by an erection on the boiler or engine-room casing. Another addition was a cabin aft for the Skipper. The biggest change came with the conversion from coal to Diesel. When one visualises the removal of the upright boiler and the installation of a Diesel power unit in place of the steam engine, the step was one of real progress, and occurred to many of the original steam, coal-fired Puffers. The bunkers were succeeded by tanks for Diesel fuel. The weight of a boiler filled with water could materially affect the trading tonnage. With the introduction of electricity, there were no navigation lights to be trimmed, but these were controlled by a switch, with power provided by a dynamo. With the conversion, it was possible to introduce much-improved crew's accommodation. A typical conversion was that of the *Kaffir*, truly a general and satisfactory transformation, with no furnace to stoke, but the engine fed by injection. The absence of coal-dust and ash were good features, and altogether the engineer must have had a much easier existence than hitherto.

Another place of Puffer construction was the Burrell Shipyard, at Hamilton Hill, near Port Dundas. Some 60 of these ships were built there, and some of them would go through the transformations already referred to. First of all, single engines, which latterly gave way to the compound type, then the inclusion of a cabin aft for the Skipper, and eventually the bridge, usually placed abaft the funnel, but sometimes in front, if space permitted.

The closing of the Forth and Clyde Canal dispensed with the restrictive measurements in Puffer construction and their somewhat 'Parochial' limits. The maximum measurements lengthwise were confined to 66 ft. to conform to the existing locks. It is not surprising that, even before its closure, Puffer owners adopted a larger vessel, which could operate through the Crinan Canal and yield increased returns. Thus the evolution continued, and now most of the successors to the Puffers are too large even for that Canal, and have to go 'Round the Mull' if proceeding to the West Highlands.

The title *Puffer Ahoy*! has been adopted so as to include waterways outside the Clyde—the cradle of ships of all sizes—and to include material of 'things that happened', for instance, the humour centring around Oban, which place, after all, was largely used by Puffers—there they would 'tie up' overnight *en route* for Crinan. Overall there were over 500 Puffers built, of various sizes.

The co-operation of many people so interested in supplying data and photographs is highly appreciated, and helpful. The personalities dealt with are true to type, and convey more fully the impressions of Puffer life. Special mention should be made of the invaluable help given by Mr. Graham E. Langmuir and Mrs. Oxford, in providing the necessary negatives and photographic prints. The author has had interesting exchange of letters with Mr. Dan McDonald, who has already had an interesting book on Puffers published.

GEORGE W. BURROWS

CONTENTS

ILLUSTRATIONS

xi

B

PUFFER AHOY!

THE ARDMORE PASSAGE

THE Ardmore Passage is situated in the Island of Islay. It was not widely used because of the prevalence of submerged rocks, which were not marked with a 'perch'. It should be explained that Ardmore is round the coast of Islay from Port Askaig, in the Sound of Islay. When the weather was stormy outside, Ardmore was calm and placid. James Burrows of the *Petrel* used to navigate this passage on occasion, being aware of the one dangerous, submerged rock. Another Puffer, the *Zephon*, which was running cargoes to and from the distilleries in Islay, had as Skipper, Jimmock Bruce, and he was said to be able to negotiate the Ardmore Channel in the dark.

Much of the Puffer trade was to and from Lagavulin, which is not far from Port Ellen. Lagavulin had a very hazardous and rocky entrance and the course to follow was, on leaving the Ardmore Channel, to keep the Channel and the *Otter* lightship in line until the large 'White Horse' on the Lagavulin building opened up to view. Then it was straight in to the Distillery jetty. The 'White Horse' distillery people had a new boat, the *Pibroch*, built by Scott & Sons, during 1923, at Bowling. She was of average size, and was engaged in carrying the commodities required in the running of the distillery, including coal, peat and barley. There were always a number of hogsheads awaiting transport to Glasgow, when the hold of the carrying vessel was sealed. There were, on occasions, attempts to remove whisky from the hogsheads when they were located on certain piers. One dodge was to lever a slot with a pocket-knife blade between two boards on the top, where there was always a recess. Once this was accomplished, the recess had water poured into it, and of course, water being of a greater density than spirits, it found its way to the bottom of the hogshead, with just that amount of spirits forced to the top. Where the whisky was stored on a timber pier, awaiting shipment, attempts were made with an auger to make a hole through the pier timber flooring, and in turn through the bottom of the hogshead!

Talking of Islay, the *Petrel* was engaged in the off-loading of about 200–300 tons of barley in sack from the coaster *Silver Springs*. The larger vessel was at a safe anchorage near Lagavulin; the *Petrel* was loaded up by her own

1

crew and derrick, making the transfer to the jetty at Lagavulin. Those engaged worked very hard, and the full bags of barley were transferred by the use of a small sling, called a 'snotter'. The bags had what looked like two ears at the top, and these were 'snottered'.

It was a tricky and hazardous coast, and the *Petrel*, on one arrival at the jetty, came to rest on the rocks, by the bow. The grounding was on a flat shelf of rock, otherwise it could have been serious. This incident was broadcast by a form of 'bush telegraph', the exaggeration reaching the proportion of TOTAL LOSS!

Incidentally, there was a small distillery near Port Ellen—Laphroaig—of which it was said that the whisky was unsurpassed, due, it was believed, to the water-finding its way via a peat bog, which gave it a unique quality.

There was a family doctor in Glasgow, a native of Taynuilt in Argyllshire, who declared, regarding the Island of Islay, that one did not require to partake of the bottled product, but rather to breathe the air, which contained an impregnation of the spirit, to obtain a high degree of satisfaction.

On the voyage from Crinan to Islay, we always had a wave from the keeper on the Mor Lighthouse, abreast of Loch Sween, which will now, no doubt, be mechanised. There was a Puffer hand who, asked about the weather, remarked, 'We got laldy-ho where we turned Ardnamurchan to go to America.'

Willie Sutherland and the author adopted a language of their own. The Skipper would suddenly take a notion to have 'dry hash' for supper, the meal consisting of potatoes, meat and a handful of oatmeal. The two members having reached the limit of digestive endurance, one or the other would remark that a number of people were taken to hospital with a serious stomach disorder, due to lack of variety of diet.

We also acquired the habit of talking in a manner only the other would understand. One would address the other thus, 'Shone Agore,' which actually meant, 'Going Ashore'—and so life went on! Incidentally, Willie had in his possession an improvised dictionary, Gaelic to English. It contained the following sentence, 'As the crow said to his feet, there are two of us.'

Willie Sutherland was identified with the Ross & Marshall boats, and at one time was Skipper of the *Sealight*. This was an older type Puffer, and as time passed, evolution in design continued, and the small coaster emerged. Typical of this was the *Raylight*, which was built in England, and provided many amenities, crew-wise, which had never before been given consideration.

Willie Sutherland was at one time with James Burrows on the *Petrel* and, having his roots in Thurso, was quite at home at Scapa Flow. Willie's death several years ago was regretted by many who had the pleasure of knowing him, and also his wife, Minnie, *née* Burrows, who also has now passed on.

The author has a small picture gallery of Puffers. Of these, one is the Larne-built Puffer *Faithful*, made fast at a jetty somewhere in the Western Isles. This is a very prized possession which became available at an auction sale at a cost of five shillings, and was suitably framed for three pounds. This Puffer is of an improved design with a carrying capacity of 120–125 tons.

Another Puffer was the *Ashdale Glen*, finally owned by Muir Brothers, Loch Long, shown in the illustration, unloading a cargo of coal into carts at Calgary, on the Island of Mull. The same owners had also a similar vessel, *Glen Finnart*. (It is interesting to note that Calgary in Canada takes its name from the Mull Calgary.)

With the beaching of a Puffer, it was an essential preliminary to carry out an inspection for the removal of large stones which could damage the vessel's hull. This was done at low tide, and guide poles placed in position, for a safe passage in. Another factor to be considered was the height of the tide, and the limit of grounding. On occasion, a Puffer has been grounded for several days, owing to tidal conditions.

Another picture is by artist Alistair Shanks, who portrays the Ross & Marshall *Starlight* at Port Ellen, Islay.

Yet another oil painting (of Inveraray Pier) indicates two eras—in the foreground is an Arran 'smack', typical of many such craft of the pre-steam era, sturdy sailing-ships with a carrying capacity of some 35 tons, and usually without an auxiliary engine. They normally had a crew of two, and were carried along by sail. The usual method of handling cargo was by a fairly large basket, which was attached on a gaff and manually operated. There was an occasion when one of these smacks, *Bee*, tied up alongside the *Petrel*, and the owner was offered a tow to Crinan, but a horse had been ordered for the transit. On this occasion, the *Petrel* had unloaded a cargo of coal for the institution locally known as the Asylum, but officially the Argyll and Bute Mental Hospital. The coal was obtained from the colliery at Campbeltown, which one does not normally associate with whisky distilleries, though there is an abundance. There is also a shipyard at Campbeltown, where cargo boats of around 8000 to 10,000 tons have been built, in an area known as the Trench.

The passage from Campbeltown to Ardrishaig was one of splendour from a naturalist's point of view, and one can recall a warm summer day, with gannets or solan geese diving with unerring precision on unsuspecting fish. The final destination was 'Millers Bridge', which provides a crossing link between Ardrishaig and Cairnbaan. There the coal cargo was discharged, and its rather poor quality would not be considered an aid to the recovery of the inmates, who were the boiler stokers and whose task it was to keep the institution heated. There was a story of a local worthy who, as the year wore on, especially in severity, had a corresponding deterioration in mental health. This person, however, had a remarkable faculty for recovery as spring weather appeared, and came into circulation again.

⚓   ⚓   ⚓   ⚓   ⚓

THE CRINAN CANAL

As is generally known, the Crinan Canal connects Ardrishaig to Crinan at the other extremity. The distance covered is approximately nine miles and dispenses with the necessity of negotiating the hazards of the Mull of Kintyre.

There are 15 locks, each approximately 95 ft. long, located at Ardrishaig, Cairnbaan, Dunardry and Crinan. There is also a number of basins, mostly circular in shape, in the course of the canal. The sea locks were renewed some years ago.

The East Reach is almost four miles long and 32 ft. above sea level and is joined with the sea at Ardrishaig by four locks and three basins. The summit reach has a length of just over 1100 yards and is 64 ft. above sea level. This, in turn, is connected with the East Reach by four locks and three basins at Cairnbaan and with the West Reach by five locks and four basins at Dunardry. The West Reach is about three miles in length and some 18 ft. above sea level, and is connected with the sea at Crinan by two locks and one basin.

The supply of stone, chiefly for the locks, came from the Isles of Arran and Mull and also from Morvern. It is interesting to note that during construction of the Canal there existed labour troubles, chiefly on account of the more advantageous terms offered in the construction of other Scottish canals and work projects in Scotland at that time.

From a navigational point of view, the stretch between Bellanoch and Crinan was the most hazardous. It was difficult because of the rocks and shallowness, and the latter could be accentuated by prolonged dry weather.

Ardrishaig always seemed to be an interesting place. There was a variety of shops, and nets from the fishing skiffs could always be seen hanging up to dry. The skiffs were seasonally engaged in the herring fishing for which

Loch Fyne was famous. Ardrishaig had one or two bakers' shops which specialised in making ship's biscuits: hard, about half an inch thick, and very palatable with a good layer of butter.

There was a daily steamer service for a period of years between Ardrishaig and Crinan. Passengers were carried the length of the Canal by the steamer *Linnet*. It was indeed possible to sail from Glasgow (Bridge Wharf) to Ardrishaig by the steamer *Columba* or *Iona* to connect with it, and from the Crinan end of the canal another MacBrayne steamer, normally (until the First World War) *Chevalier*, continued to Oban. In summer it was usually the *Columba* which made the run to Ardrishaig; and it was during this run in the mornings that the memorable competition race took place for Gourock pier. Some of the steamers involved were the *Columba, Ivanhoe, Lord of the Isles* and several of the railway ships. With the stokers working 'full tilt', and with black smoke from the funnels, it was a sight not to be forgotten.

MacBraynes had a cargo steamer, *Brenda* (virtually a large Puffer) which had a regular run between Glasgow and the West Highlands. This ship, being 84 ft. in length and of suitable draught, could make the canal passage, which she did with great regularity, calling at ports on the west side of Knapdale and Lorne, Oban, Fort William, Loch Sunart, etc. The Captain of the *Linnet* was immaculately dressed in a navy blue serge suit with brass buttons, and he was daily to the fore, resplendent in a white shirt. It happened that the *Petrel* was at the canal basin at Crinan and was approaching the *Linnet* broadside. A nephew of the *Petrel's* Skipper, against emphatic orders to the contrary, threw a heaving line which landed fair and square on the white shirt front. The language which followed from James Burrows was unprintable!

The Canal Company had the *Conway*, a specially adapted icebreaker— with a continuous spell of frost, ice could be a distinct hazard. She was used on occasion as an 'overflow' vessel for passengers who could not be accommodated on the *Linnet*, as also was the MacBrayne Puffer *Countess of Kellie*.

It took around five hours for a fully-laden Puffer to negotiate the passage when the Canal Authorities had resident lock-keepers to assist a ship through the Canal; but, since the economy axe was wielded, the time for the passage has taken longer. A loaded Puffer with a draught in excess of 9 ft. going from Bellanoch Bridge and Crinan, had difficulties owing to the lack of water, especially in the summer season. Such a vessel was the Leith-built *Inchcolm*, which had a draught of somewhere around 10–11 ft. when fully loaded. Incidentally, Bellanoch Bay is regarded as one of the beauty spots in the Crinan Canal.

Before the new and improved sea lock was in operation, the original basin formed a harbour of refuge, mostly for wind-bound Puffers. Storm conditions could last for days on end, and an increasing degree of frustration was apparent among the Skippers and crews. Of course there was quite a prevalence of rabbits, pheasants, etc., and these fellows did not always consult as to what was the 'off' season! There was always an odd gun, and some of the boys were expert in snaring. Where game birds were roosting in the trees in the evening, sometimes a sulphur fire was kindled underneath them on the ground, with fatal results only, of course, to the pheasants. Then there was the eminence which rose up beside the basin at Crinan, where there was always a good rabbit population; and adders were not unknown during the summer and autumn. The Puffer men lived quite high, food-wise, and at no great personal expense! Many a good meal was contained in a large frying-pan, which was placed on a protective newspaper on the fo'c'sle table. Then followed a free for all which was, in the main, orderly! The boys were never short of ham and eggs, and never appeared to be in any sense emaciated. The question of balance was maintained by fish, which could be sea trout with perhaps an occasional salmon. These were netted overnight at selected spots.

On several occasions when Puffers were alongside each other in the Crinan Basin and awaiting moderation in the weather, frustration increased daily. On one of the boats (not the *Sterlina*) many of the crew members and Skippers of the other Puffers were assembled in the fo'c'sle indulging in accounts of their intrepid bravery in difficult situations. Nobody seemed to hear a bootless figure on the deck above, but the detonation of a handful of gunpowder down the stove chimney resulted in no small measure of confusion. Stove lids flew about the place and soot was everywhere. This would have to happen after the hinged table and seats had been beautifully scrubbed down. These fo'c'sles were mostly kept in very good condition. There was a sense of frustration at the delay of being stormbound. Today the resultant prankish action might be called vandalism—who can decide?

During the First World War a new group of internal-combustion-engined boats had been built, all with names beginning with *Innis*. The *Innisdhu* hove into sight at Crinan *en route* from Ardrishaig. She did not, however, join the other Puffers at the basin, but successfully negotiated the sea-lock and proceeded on her way. The strong winds still persisted and the sea lock was again filled when in came the *Innisdhu*, skippered by that memorable figure, James Froud, in appearance very similar to the mythical 'Captain Kettle', with bearded face and outstanding chin. The *Innisdhu* proceeded canal-wise to Ardrishaig, *en route* for Glasgow, where she arrived and was reloaded. She duly re-appeared at Ardrishaig, and made the Canal passage to Crinan. In view of many red faces, Froud again went on his way. Shortly after this the weather moderated, and one by one the other Puffers took their departure. It should be borne in mind that the type of engine installed in the *Innisdhu* had reached no great stage of reliability, and breakdowns were fairly frequent. At that time there was speculation as to which boat had carried away the end of Colintraive Pier, Kyles of Bute, with a query on Froud of the *Innisdhu*!

Another Puffer with Crinan Canal associations was the *Tiree*—a fairly regular trader. The usual cargo from Glasgow terminus was coal, and the *Tiree* would proceed Crinan-wise, gradually beginning to look fresher with the application of buckets of water. Her Skipper always made himself presentable between Ardlamont Point and Ardrishaig and, as the Canal was approached, as nearly immaculate as a Puffer Skipper could be. He always took the wheel on the Canal passage, and was most polite to ladies walking on the bank, but, on occasion, he forgot that he was steering a Puffer in a restricted inland waterway. The result was that the *Tiree* would slew round and be more or less across the Canal! She was not very fast and some wag suggested that the name should be 'Tired'.

There was a Puffer, the Skipper of which was obsessed with the apparent lack of vacuum registered on the engine-room gauge. He would keep reiterating that the engine was running short of vacuum. This reached a stage where J. Hill, the somewhat aged engineer, was annoyed and sought a cure. The Skipper was in a vantage position, where the vacuum gauge could be seen, and he was pleasantly surprised to see a much higher reading on the gauge. What Jock Hill had done was to dismantle the vacuum gauge in which was contained a quadrant. This Hill successfully manipulated so that when the engine was stopped, several inches of vacuum was registered. It was some time before the Skipper was aware of this, and when he was—his language could have put the gauge back from shock!

Then there was the story of the Owner/Skipper of a Puffer, which shall at the moment be unidentified. The Puffer was in the region of the Mull of Kintyre, which at times is referred to as the 'graveyard of Puffers'. The situation had reached the stage where the small boat was afloat. The Skipper and his crew had rowed some distance away, when a crew member noticed that the engineer was at the stern, waving frantically for help. He had been below when the others took off. The crew member said to the Skipper, 'We've left Alec behind.' The Skipper replied, 'Pull away, boys, it'll look better for the insurance if there is one drowned.' As stated, this was the story, the reader can form his or her opinion as to its veracity!

There was also a Puffer Owner and Skipper who had difficulty in obtaining his freight money for the cargoes carried. The intermediary was the broker, and on this particular occasion he was anything but accommodating. The Puffer Owner had commitments, running expenses, etc., and was finally ordered or pushed away from the broker's office, the door of which was in course of being shut. The Puffer Owner was elderly; but not short of spirit for, on the stairway, he set about tearing his shirt and scratching himself to the effusion of blood. In the resultant distressed state, he sought out the police and was listened to sympathetically about the alleged assault. The case eventually went to court and the 'assaulted' one explained to the magistrate, 'I'm just a puir auld man trying to make an honest living, and ye ken, My Lord, this man refused to pay me, and pushed me doon the stairs.' The old man could successfully put on the act, and had the court on his side!

There is also the cash-on-delivery story of a Puffer which carried a cargo of coal and the 'Old Man' was contemplating passing the anchor chain around the wheel of the locomotive, to discourage the removal of the loaded trucks until payment was made.

There were two Puffers, well kept and maintained, owned by Colin McPhail, the *Gleannshira* and *Stronshira*. The former was built by Scotts of Bowling, and the other had been previously named *North Inch* and *Garmoyle*: she was one of two Dumbarton-built vessels which 'loaded by the heid', and which maintained the reputation of imbalance. Incidentally, it is surprising that a firm located at Dumbarton, with all its accumulated knowledge, could produce such 'off-trim' craft. They were, however, beyond reproach in other aspects of shipbuilding.

Brief mention has been made of the machinery or power unit installed in many of the Puffers around the early years of this century. Larger-carrying capacity called for increased power. The firm of Gauldie & Gillespie were in the forefront, and they produced a compound unit with cylinder diameter of 12 in. on the high-pressure side, and 22 in. low pressure, the engine stroke being 16 in. The power unit also operated air, feed and circulation pumps and there was also a separate donkey pump which could be used for general service, such as boiler injection and deck washing.

The boiler was of upright type, 12 ft. high and about 6 ft. diameter, with several cross-tubes above the fire-box. It should, incidentally, be mentioned that James Burrows, with his Larne-built Puffer, held the opinion that the high-pressure cylinder would create more efficiency if the bore was reduced to 10 in. He arranged to have a liner fitted. The alteration made proved to have negative results, because the balance was disturbed. Such considerations were better left to the designers, who had the experience or 'know-how'.

Competitively, the *Petrel* never held sway speed-wise after the insertion of the high-pressure cylinder liner, and the title of speediest Puffer in that class passed to the *Rivercloy*, which was built at Larne for George Hamilton of Brodick. Together with his brother Gavin, he considered the Puffer business seriously, and had arrangements for the continuity of cargo transport outward from and inward to the upper Clyde. With regard to the *Rivercloy*, George Hamilton had a theory that, in building at Larne, an extra foot should be added to the 'bluff' of the bows. The theory was that widening at that part ensured less resistance.

As mentioned on another page, the Ayrshire-built *Warlight* (Ross & Marshall) outpaced all others and was the fastest Puffer afloat. She could just pass through the Crinan Canal without cargo, and was a tight fit length-wise in the locks.

In much the same degree, the *Jennie* and the *Ormsa* were maintained by the well-known personage, Malcolm Campbell, who had two sons, Duncan and Alex. Each was in charge of a vessel: Duncan was Skipper of the *Ormsa* and Alex of the *Jennie*. These Puffers were fitted with compound surface condensing engines, but the *Jennie* was noteworthy for the installation of quite a heavy flywheel, fitted in a central position on the crankshaft.

As the function of the flywheel is to store up energy, one wonders just how the power unit was controlled, especially when a change of direction was required. Unfortunately the *Jennie* was eventually lost by running aground on the Island of Eigg during foggy weather. All three Campbells, father and two sons, are buried in Kirkmichael Churchyard, not far from Ardrishaig.

These Puffers had the usual hull design with rudder and either a three- or four-bladed propeller. Incidentally, vessels such as those built at Larne had wooden masts and derricks, selected from pitch pine trees. These spars were not lathe-turned; but had hand treatment with an adze and a large spokeshave, used by expert tradesmen. The later Puffers were equipped with steel masts.

The derrick was fitted with a type of swivel joint, sometimes referred to as a 'gooseneck' (a forging which was specially made to suit and which would operate up and down and also sideways). The name 'derrick' originated from a hangman of the 17th century, whose lethal apparatus had a similar construction to the ship's derrick as used at present.

The derrick was used in canal work on the Forth and Clyde and Crinan Canals, and it was used for a member of the crew to swing to and from the vessel after a set of locks or a bridge were negotiated, and there followed a 'reach' of up to four miles without obstruction. (It was a rule that a crew member had to lend a hand in the operation of locks and bridges.)

At least one Puffer carried a 'gin' or 'sleeve', of mild steel, about 5 ft. long, in two halves, which were clamped to the derrick at the weakest point under load, and was employed when heavy lifts were in progress.

About this time in the evolution of Puffers, the Board of Trade introduced certain safety measures, including a safety wire-rope connected between the mast and derrick. This, in fact, served as a possible check when under load, and through wear or neglect, the derrick ropes or falls became unsafe, and a break might occur, with serious results.

⚓   ⚓   ⚓   ⚓   ⚓

THE TWO TEAPOTS

IT is a well-known fact that Puffer men enjoy a mug of tea: it is the staff of life to them. When the weather is wild and the seas are running high, the tea very often was brewed in cold water in a pan and brought to the boil, provided the pan would remain on the stove-top! Condensed milk and sugar were added to taste, and there this procedure provided a mug of tea, excellently palatable to the consumer.

The 'Two Teapots' were two men, father and son. The father was deformed, and his stature suggested something akin to a teapot. He was a very good engine- and boiler-man, and his shape seemed to lend itself to stoking the boiler successfully. Where a normal, tall, robust man would have to stoop low for a shovelful of coal, the 'Teapot' could take it in his stride.

When the 'Teapot's' son became active in the Puffers, he quickly assumed the name, the 'Blazing Teapot'. There had to be a distinguishing factor, and this was it. He also became efficient as an engineer and boiler-man, and vied favourably in a race with his father when the occasion arose.

It should be stated that the upright boiler was exposed to the engine unit, there being no protective bulkhead, the cleaning of the boiler-fire being a distinct source of dust and ash. Incidentally, a well-built Puffer was a fine craft in quite a heavy sea. Loaded, there was little or no freeboard, and the afterpart could be almost awash. A personal recollection is of a Puffer travelling light, having its two large unloading buckets (capacity 5 cwts), tossed from one end of the hold to the other, when the ship left the leeway of the south of the Island of Kerrera to the open water of the Atlantic Ocean, almost abreast of Easdale Island.

⚓   ⚓   ⚓   ⚓   ⚓

KELVINDOCK, MARYHILL
AND CRAFT ON THE FORTH AND CLYDE CANAL
Contributed by the late C. A. McNICOLL

PRIOR to Maryhill being annexed by Glasgow, it was a burgh, having its own Magistrates, Police Force, etc., and prior to its being a burgh it was a village which came into being with the completion of the Forth and Clyde Canal from Stockingfield to Bowling. The district was usually referred to as Drydock, the Dock or Kelvindock before being named Kelvindock, Maryhill. *A Companion for Canal Passengers Betwixt Edinburgh and Glasgow*, published in 1823, mentions that a short distance north from Stockingfield, Port Kelvin is pointed out by the numerous masts of ships which, with surprise, are here observed on the top of an eminence far from the sea. From this it would appear that the intention of the Canal Company had been to call the area around the locks Port Kelvin, but, with a large number of men permanently employed at the drydock, and with no other name for the area, it was natural to refer to the place as indicated above. However, Maryhill got its present name, and the graving dock became known as Kelvindock.

Being too tall when I left school to get a job as an office boy, and unsuccessful in being accepted as an apprentice in a drawing-office, I commenced work as an apprentice shipwright at Kelvindock, where my father was Manager and my brother worked as a shipwright.

A little elaboration of the work carried out and some mention of the vessels using the Canal or built in the drydock might not be without interest, now that the Forth and Clyde Canal is closed.

But first a word about 'that chain of masonwork consisting of locks, basins, drydock and bridges' and to quote the *Scots Magazine* of 1789, when all the work was completed, 'That stupendous bridge, the great aqueduct over the river Kelvin,' which they reckoned was pre-eminent over anything of a similar nature in Europe. Certainly 'Neptune's Stairway', consisting of the aqueduct and the locks, is a striking instance of the power of human industry, and seems more so today when we visit them and ponder on the lack of mechanical means in the building of them.   The Aqueduct and the Locks stand today as a monument to the engineering skill of the designer and the craftsmanship of the masons who did the work.   No wonder people have come from all over the world to view this architecture.

Of course there were no thoughts like that in my mind that first morning when I started work, wearing dungarees over my knickerbockers, and I was told to get a tar brush and do some tarring on the bottom of a lighter about to be undocked.   I was next sent to 'Bump the Hobby' for 'Baldy'.   My wonder as to what sort of job that might be, and the alliteration, still makes me smile. 'Baldy' was the holder on to a squad of riveters, and when he could not get his big, holding-on hammer on the head of a rivet, he resorted to a suitably-shaped iron bar, or hobby, the end of which he held on the rivet head, and the rivet-boy, the writer in this case, held the big holding hammer on the other end of the hobby, and bumped when necessary.

Placed where it is, between the two locks, the graving dock is unique in that no pump is required to empty it, as the water can be run off by means of a sluice to a basin on the lower level.   Nor is it dependent on the tide-level water and can be used at any time.   The water level could also be brought higher by fitting temporary, heavy wooden boards on the lock gates.   This was rather a tricky operation, requiring one man to hang well over into the lock, holding on by one hand while swinging the board into place with the other. There is little wonder that no one was very keen on the job!

The graving Dock is approximately 150 ft. long and could dock at the same time, two of the largest-size vessels using the Canal.   Alongside the dry dock and skirting Maryhill Road there was a long, tiled, open-fronted shed containing a saw-pit.

Before Maryhill had a church, religious services were occasionally held here, the saw-pit being covered over with planks, and the congregation sat or stood in the shed.

I would be one of the last persons to assist in the use of the saw-pit for cutting timber, my job being in the pit at the bottom end of the two-man saw. The shed is gone now and the ground occupied by it, taken in to widen Maryhill Road.

Great care was taken when docking a boat, and in cold and dirty weather it could be quite unpleasant, as the heavy wooden shores and blocks used in the job were all handled manually.

Many an unusual type of vessel has been gently cradled in the old dry dock in order to heal her wounds or spruce her up.

Vessels from the Continent were occasional visitors, one of the most welcome of which I would imagine to be the Dutch smack, whose Captain sat on deck each morning and issued a tot of rum to his crew and all who were working on his ship.

The first ever iron vessel, *Vulcan*, passed the dock frequently and no doubt, on occasion, paid it a visit.

As well as doing repair work, building was carried on, and many scows, lighters, gabbarts, barges and Puffers were built at Kelvindock. These would be of wood until about the middle of last century, when the last wooden vessel, a smack called the *Osprey*, was built there. She would be among the last of this type of vessel built for the coastal trade and, along with one or two other similar craft, caused much interest any time they arrived in the Canal, with their long bowsprits heaved up to clear the lock gates. Their tall masts, with perhaps a yard across, the rigging, the long wooden tiller, the small hatches, clean bulwarks and decks, all giving an air of having come from far-off places.

After the successful advent of the *Vulcan*, shipbuilders soon turned to iron for the construction of hulls, and it would seem that Kelvindock did not lag far behind in that respect, being soon well equipped with furnaces and machinery for dealing with iron hulls. Long hours, hard work and no demarcation were the order of the day, and what better training could a boy have than experience in the various branches of the work? One of the firms which operated the drydock in its early days also started shipbuilding on the south bank of the Canal at Maryhill, launching into the top basin, between the docks.

Vessels too large to pass through the Canal were built in two or three sections here, floated down to Dumbarton and re-assembled there. The firm later opened a yard at Dumbarton for the building of these larger vessels, and it is interesting to note that the first vessel built, the *Fitzmaurice*, was partly fabricated at Kelvindock. This was the vessel that found the cylinder or pontoon, containing 'Cleopatra's Needle' drifting in the Bay of Biscay, abandoned in a storm by the tug which had been towing it to England; and she towed the pontoon into Vigo on the coast of Spain.

Launching the smaller vessels built at Kelvindock was usually a spectacular affair, as the majority were launched broadside into the dock, which caused a mighty splash. They could also launch end-on into the basin between the locks, in which case the vessel slipped quietly into the water without fuss. But, whatever method was used, it was always done in style, with flags, ribbons, the bottle and sponsor: an occasion for rejoicing for a job well done, and the excuse for a dram!

Vulcan, the first iron vessel, was built at Faskine, on the Monkland Canal and designed for the passenger traffic on the Forth and Clyde Canal. Later she was rigged with sails, and 45 years after being launched, she was doing duty as a barge on the Canal, which speaks well of her construction. I remember listening to my father describe the construction of the *Vulcan*, which he had seen lying derelict somewhere in the Canal.

Smacks and gabbarts were hauled by horses when on the Canal, but used their sails when on the river or firth and, as they had no deck machinery other than a small windlass for discharging the cargo: this was a slow process, often when the cargo was coal, involving baskets passed from hand to hand as being the quickest method. It is interesting to note that horses were still used on the Forth and Clyde Canal until well into the Second World War, when the scows and barges that they moved were taken over by the Government for use elsewhere.

Early attempts were made to introduce steam propulsion on the Forth and Clyde Canal, and in 1857 there were five screw steamers daily at work on the Canal. These then would be the forerunners of the ubiquitous Puffer, known all over the world, and now, themselves, practically extinct.

From a lighter or scow, with perhaps an open hatch and no bulwarks, the Puffer developed into a sturdy vessel, still able to use the Forth and Clyde Canal, carrying up to 125 tons of cargo, with a speed of about seven knots, and able to go anywhere around the coasts and across to Ireland.

Screw lighters of various sizes and for various owners were built to suit the Canal and coasting trade and, until well past the middle of last century, these were mostly built at Kelvindock and at Blackhill, on the Monkland Canal. One great improvement came with the steam engine for propulsion—the use of a steam winch for operating the cargo derrick, lifting the anchor, warping the vessel, etc. Thus the Puffer was able to go where there were no facilities for handling cargoes, especially those of a heavy nature, and to do so expeditiously.

I am sure it will surprise many to know that, apart from fog and ice, the Canal had other navigation difficulties, such as during strong winds when it was difficult, sometimes impossible, to handle a 'light' Puffer safely, while a loaded scow with its low freeboard and open hold crossing the wide area of the bog at Dullatur, could easily be swamped by the large waves there.

During both World Wars, the Forth and Clyde Canal Puffer was found to be a most useful vessel, and during World War I several were stationed at Scapa Flow, and were used for carrying stores, water, ammunition, etc., to the various ships of the fleet. During World War II, the demand for their services repeated itself to a much greater extent, and many were built by the Admiralty for use in home waters. Also, many were shipped to almost every overseas base under British control.

Kelvindock also played its part during both World Wars, being taken over by Inland Water Transport during the First World War, when most of the scows were taken over and fitted with tanks for transporting oil from the Clyde to Grangemouth.

Scows were barges small enough to use the Monkland Canal, decked at the forward and aft ends and for a width of about 12 to 15 in. on either side of the open hold.

The business at Kelvindock was taken over by my brother and myself in 1922. He had been Manager there since 1909, and during the Second World War, Kelvindock was once more taken over by the Admiralty and a roof fitted over the drydock, so that work could be carried out there in all weathers. The yard then became a centre for the repair and refitting of troop- and tank-carrying landing craft damaged in action. Hundreds of these craft were thus dealt with in the dock, and on the yacht slip adjoining the dry dock.

The last craft built at Kelvindock were two steel yachts, both of which were shipped overseas.

With the Forth and Clyde Canal now closed, the craft used for work in the Canal only, that is the horse-drawn scows and lighters, the steam lighters with their 'thief hole' in the engine-room bulkhead, so that the cargo of coal might be available in the event of the bunker coal giving out, and the Puffer with its dimensions restricted to suit the Canal, are no more. (The thief hole was a doorway to the hold from the engine-room or stokehold. It does not appear that such access was gained only in an emergency, but in a deliberate attempt to filch the coal cargo. Many of the customers raised objections and gradually the 'hole' was closed up, and not left as an access in later Puffers.) However the memory of the Puffer lives on in the larger sizes now being built for coastal work, and fitted with Diesel engines, Radar navigational equipment, automatic heating, washing machine, refrigerator and gas cooker for the crew.

So much for Kelvindock and the various types of craft using the Forth and Clyde Canal, but what of the men who built and manned the vessels? Many of the tradesmen in Kelvindock would, of course, be boys who had served their apprenticeship in the local yard. Some would come from other yards

C

building larger vessels, and not a few of the shipwrights had been all over the world in sailing-vessels, bringing back with them stories of their experiences.

The carpenter of the famous tea-clipper *Thermopylae* was a frequent visitor. Old Tom Smith, while whale fishing in Arctic waters, saw the boat in which his father was one of the crew smashed to matchwood by the tail of a whale, and everyone killed. Tom also had the experience of a Russian prison, not for any crime that he had committed personally, but apparently because of the ship's whaling activities.

The ship carpenters working at Kelvindock held an Annual Supper and Ball, which sometimes took place in the drawing-loft of the yard or in a local hall. It is interesting to note that the supper at these functions was opened by the singing of a psalm, followed by a prayer, and it closed with a prayer. I was told by a man who had attended one of these functions that, during the evening, more water was required for making toddy but, as the well from which the water was obtained was on the other side of the Canal, and no one being in a fit state to negotiate the crossing by the lock gate, it was decided to use whisky instead of water, and not take risks!

⚓   ⚓   ⚓   ⚓   ⚓

KELVINDOCK (MARYHILL)

THE name McNicoll is synonymous with Puffer construction. The McNicoll brothers and their father built ships of which they were proud. The Puffers which were built at Kelvindock could be relied on for good, solid construction, and the correct trim when afloat.

The *Kype* and *Logan* were a pair to the order of Dickson & Co., and these two boats would carry 120 tons of cargo. Another boat built by them was the *Hafton*, but she was not of such a big-carrying capacity.

Towards the end of last century, a shipyard came into being at Larne, in Northern Ireland, and quite a number of Puffers were built there. About the first of these was to the order of James Burrows, and was named *Petrel*. Then followed a number of others: *Jennie, Jessie, Lythe, Faithful*, and two of the later ones, the *Ormsa* and *Rivercloy*, which was built in 1902.

Regarding the boatyard at Hamilton Hill, Port Dundas, owned by Burrell & Co., a typical example of its products was the *Dorothy*, built in 1901, afterwards owned by J. Hay & Co. She was a very tidy craft, and was a good carrier.

Scott & Sons of Bowling also built many Puffers, quite a number for

Paton & Hendry, all to the same design. The *Zephon* was a typical example of the Bowling yard's output.

Another Scott production was the *Invercloy*, built to the order of the Hamilton Brothers of Arran in 1904. This was a nice craft, well maintained and together with the Larne-built *Rivercloy*, well known in the Western Islands.

Ross & Marshall had quite a big fleet of 'Puffers', known as the 'Lights': *Sealight, Stormlight, Moonlight, Starlight,* etc. The crew of the *Starlight,* the Dewars, were well known with their Easdale connection, and became famous for the breeding of canaries.

Easdale was always an attractive place within easy reach of Oban: many visitors went to the Island to partake of the home-baking and afternoon teas. At one time the sea anemones were a beautiful feature at the pier at Easdale, the water at the pier being so clear that it was delightful to view these creatures of nature. Easdale was not without its industry—slate quarrying—and there was also one factory which produced furniture.

THE FORTH AND CLYDE CANAL

THE Forth and Clyde Canal has an historical place in inland navigation, chiefly because of its length of almost 40 miles, with some 40 locks from Grangemouth to its extremity at Port Dundas in the one direction and at Bowling at the other end, the junction being at Stockingfield, which is subject to stormy winds.

The total cost of the Canal was reckoned to be around £200,000, which, towards the end of the 17th century, would be regarded as considerable. No doubt labour was plentiful and it would be an interesting conjecture as to the average weekly earnings of a workman in those days. There would be the navvy and the stonemason. One must regard the mass of stonework involved, especially at Maryhill and Kelvin, which has long-been regarded, nationally and internationally, as an attractive feature of the Canal. Altogether many hundreds of men must have been employed in the construction of this waterway.

The Canal is, on the average, quite wide—60 ft. at water level and 30 ft. at bottom; and, with regard to its depth, it was possible for two fully-loaded Puffers, drawing about $9\frac{1}{2}$ ft., to pass each other without much difficulty.

Most of the craft at the opening, and for many years were horsedrawn and of wood. Then, in 1818, the first iron boat appeared. This was the *Vulcan* (built on the Monkland Canal), which could carry some 200 passengers and their luggage.

Passenger traffic had not been neglected and a private company (to whom the lease had been given in 1852), in 1860, introduced the screw steamer *Rockvilla Castle*, which was still in operation in 1883 and was the last passenger steamer on the Canal to give service runs. In 1893 the first *Fairy Queen* was commissioned for excursions only, with accommodation for 200 passengers. The journey was made between Kirkintilloch and Port Dundas. The *Fairy Queen* was pleasing to the eye, and was to a degree popular—evening cruises were arranged from Kirkintilloch to Craigmarloch, and then to the terminal at Port Dundas. As time passed, the *Fairy Queen* was inadequate to cope with the increased passenger traffic, and she was succeeded by the second *Fairy Queen*. The passenger cruises increased in popularity, and this ship was augmented in 1903 by the *May Queen*, graceful in her build and with more covered accommodation. The last steamship to engage in the passenger trade was the *Gipsy Queen*, considerably larger than the *May Queen*. These vessels were owned by James Aitken & Co. Ltd., Kirkintilloch. The *Gipsy Queen* was utilitarian and non-graceful in appearance. However, she was well appointed for the comfort of the passengers. Mostly at the wheel on the *Gipsy Queen* was Captain Aitken, and the pleasant sound of the dynamo engine could often be heard in the hours of darkness.

The popularity of the passenger trade was maintained until the outbreak of war in 1914, when the Canal came under Government control. The *Fairy Queen* had been disposed of in 1912 and the *May Queen* in 1918. A smaller motor-vessel, *Fairy Queen (III)* was added in 1923. These somewhat legendary ships passed not without leaving a pleasant memory. They had an escort of boys, who would race along the tow-path and perform cartwheels. Coppers were thrown by the passengers, not without mishap to the boys on occasion. The journey commencing at Port Dundas and terminating at Craigmarloch, did not involve the use of locks *en route*.

At that time, the author lived in a house overlooking the Forth and Clyde Canal and this engendered a familiarity with regard to the traffic.

There was a family named Geddes, who acted in the recovery of the victims of drowning fatalities at the Forth and Clyde Canal, and also in the Clyde harbour. Geordie Geddes was the head of the family, and would appear at the Canal or Harbour dressed as a Captain, with skip cap and navy-blue serge suit and a white shirt. At Canal recovery operations, his well-kept rowing-boat was usually pulled along the Canal from Port Dundas by a few boys until the dreaded spot was reached.   Then the grappling irons were used for the recovery of the body.   It is assumed that the rescue operations also included the Monkland Canal.

There were many companies having boats of the Puffer type on the Canal. The *Annie* and *Nellie* were two smart and trim craft which operated between Port Dundas and Falkirk.   When the days were seasonably short, these vessels would make their way along with navigation lights.   There were also Carron boats which had numbers.   They had a regular trade between Port Dundas, Falkirk and Grangemouth.

Then there was quite a fleet owned by James Currie & Co., commonly known as the Leith boats.   They did not have names, as such, but instead, were distinguished by a letter of the alphabet.   There would be the '*O*' of Leith or the '*X*' of Leith, and each had rather a long funnel with the Currie Line colours of black with white band.   They were propelled by a type of diagonal engine and horizontal boilers.   Around 1923, these Leith boats were in process of being disbanded, and at least three of them, '*X*', '*Z*' and '*O*', became privately owned on the Clyde.   Being designed for Canal traffic, they were rather unsuited for the open waters of the Clyde coasts, where stormy weather was often the order of the day.   They did not have a big carrying capacity, possibly some 60–80 tons.

There were occasions when large, marine boilers and triple-expansion engines had to be transported from the Clyde to the East Coast.   Certain Puffers had a wide and long hatch, and these boats were loaded mostly by the Finnieston crane.   For easy unloading, the heavy wire slings and shackles were left in position.

There was an interesting situation where a Canal aqueduct spans what is now Maryhill Road.   On occasion a large Puffer could be seen from the road making the Canal passage.   One wonders just how often some of these vessels, fully loaded, would touch the bottom of the aqueduct and require mechanical means to move them.   In any case, it was with no little measure of surprise and a certain amount of eye-rubbing, that viewers saw a Puffer crossing the road!

In those days, Canal boatmen, and indeed many other workers, wore white moleskin trousers, and one old-timer remarked to me that they added something to a picturesque scene when working their boat through the waterway.

The men who manned the Puffers would, of course, have gravitated from the smacks and gabbarts, but there was also an experienced leaven of sailors from the oceans of the world.   They were a hardy breed, as they had to be working their vessels in all kinds of bad weather and in difficult places. They could relate experiences which would make lovers of the tales of 'Para-Handy' admit that 'truly, truth is stranger than fiction'.

I knew a Skipper and heard him tell the tale of how, with his penknife, he amputated the badly-smashed finger of his engineer, after their Puffer had been stormbound for several days in an inaccessible Highland loch. This was necessary because the finger was becoming gangrenous and no doctor or local help was available.

The story is also true of the Puffer whose crew dropped anchor near Leith harbour and, leaving the vessel unmanned, rowed ashore for a dram. While sitting in the tavern, the crew saw a local tug boat go alongside the abandoned Puffer, lift her anchor, tow her into dock and moor her alongside the tug. This was a serious matter, having their vessel salvaged in this way, and the crew were in a quandary. However, as they watched, they saw the crew of the tug-boat preparing to depart, presumably to their homes, which eventually they did. The Puffer's crew then slipped on board their own boat, cast off the mooring ropes and proceeded on their way. It would have been interesting to have heard the comments of the tug-boat crew when they returned and found that their prize had vanished!

There was always a friendly rivalry between the various Skippers and crews as to what they, and their boats could do, and many races were held if two or more boats were making for the same port. One of the fastest Puffers was built at Kelvindock, and she was reputed to be able to do the journey from Belfast to Bowling on the Clyde several hours faster than any of the others. The boat was named *Gnome*, and was skippered at one time by Richard Burrows.

To see from a headland a tiny Puffer with its 120 tons of coal, pushing its way slowly on towards an Irish or Hebridean port was, I always thought, sufficient to justify a 'Well done, wee boat.'

As a final note on the 'Dock', it is interesting to recall a remark made to the writer many years ago by a Maryhill lady who was in a position to know, that the first building in Maryhill was the wall around the head of the Drydock.

The writer of the foregoing notes, C. A. McNicoll, was the last person to serve an apprenticeship as a shipwright at Kelvindock. The thorough training received there stood him in good stead later as a ship's draughtsman and Assistant Yard Manager on the Clyde, and later as Superintendent in charge of shipbuilding and repairs in a large Canadian shipyard.

A derisory wish of dislike was, 'Southerly wind in your bag or sail.' This could be said either jokingly or in earnest.

The firm of Jack & Co. also had at least two Puffers, which were often engaged in Canal work. They were the *Boer* and the *Afghan*. They had black funnels and a touch of green above the water-line. The firm of Jack had a number of scows. These were of the barge type, and without any mechanical propulsion. They were usually drawn, loaded, by one strong horse, and often carried sawn timber planks of various lengths to the sawmills along the Canal. The horse was usually muzzled to prevent feeding along the Canal bank.

The firm of J. & J. Hay, later J. Hay & Co., also had many scows, and they had facilities for building Puffers and scows at their shipyard at Kirkintilloch, as also had P. McGregor & Co. at their neighbouring yard. The type of Puffer which Hay & Co. built was practical, but, by reason of the extra belting on the bow, was not graceful.

There were a number of horse-drawn lighters owned by James Rankine & Son. These were in every way superior to the scows already mentioned, with better accommodation for the crew. As they could carry a load of approximately 80 tons, it took two strong horses to pull them. In the same way as the scows, they were often used for Scandinavian or Baltic timber in planks or battens.

In later years there was a tanker lighter, *Perfection*, propelled by an internal combustion engine. It plied between Port Dundas and Grangemouth.

There were a number of works along the Canal, one of which was Mark Hurll's Brickwork at Temple, near Anniesland. This firm supplied quite a few cargoes for the Western Isles. It was not uncommon to see a Puffer with a cylindrical land boiler in tow, possibly for a Western Isles distillery.

The present Bantaskin Street, which used to be referred to as Botany Brae, figured in various incidents over the years. As the name suggests, this was the Brae which joined the Main Street, now part of Maryhill Road. It has been suggested that this was an assembly point for convicts *en route* for Botany Bay in Australia. They were assembled and conveyed in groups, presumably to Bowling, where in turn they joined the ship which was bound for Australia.

No one can imagine the privations and the ordeal of many of these convicts, who were taken from various prisons in Britain because the accommodation in the prisons became so limited. Many were thrown into prison as the result of stealing a loaf of bread in order to survive. Men, women and children were involved, and the journey to Botany Bay was an ordeal which many did not survive. The voyage took several months, and the name Botany Bay would suggest a delectable spot. The reverse was the case and they faced a future of extreme hardship and tortuous conditions. There is nothing to substantiate the story of the 'Brae', but it has always been known as 'Botany', and there could be a link.

There was a factory of some type so far down the Brae where it was planned to instal a land boiler, and in due course the boiler arrived at the Brae head. Arrangements were made to 'anchor' the tackle and render the boiler down, bit by bit. It appears that so far down, the considerable weight asserted itself and the boiler was out of control. It careered downhill towards the location shed, demolished the gable-end, and landed only a matter of inches from its desired position. It is not on record that anyone suffered injury.

⚓   ⚓   ⚓   ⚓   ⚓

ABOUT OBAN

THE local excursion steamer, *Princess Louise*, on occasion brought sheep to Oban cattle sales. The sheep were going up the gangway, and as the last animal disappeared, the shepherd was heard to say, 'Iss there no more sheep on board but me?'

There is the story of the Oban town crier of bygone days. It was on a Saturday evening and events for the coming Lord's Day were being dealt with. No doubt the town crier had been in the company of friends, because his announcement was to the effect that 'The Grenadier will preach in the Free Church and the Minister will go round Staffa and Iona.'

The ramifications of Mrs. Henrietta Spencer and Donald MacQueen are worthy of mention. Their running of pleasure-boats to interesting places was always a feature of Oban. Mrs. Spencer was, and is, a personality in Oban. With her nautical appearance and tanned, weatherbeaten face, she could easily be mistaken for a man. Her knowledge of the waters around Oban and, of course, the peculiar tide movements, are par excellence. Times without number, Mrs. Spencer and Donald MacQueen have made the journey over to Grass Point and Craignure, and they have kept the Isle of Mull up to date with newspapers and mail, as well as other goods of many descriptions. Mrs. Spencer's activities were not always confined to the pleasure-boat side and at one time she owned a sailing cargo auxiliary which took her much farther away.

Mention might be made of the anchorage at Dunstaffnage–Benderloch area where convoys of ships were assembled during the last war. It was regarded as a safe anchorage until a ship suffered an underwater attack and became submerged. It was stated at the time that there was a number of valuable racehorses on board. One of these horses was seen, swimming off Dunstaffnage Castle, by a young woman, who courageously swam out and brought the horse and an accompanying dog ashore. It was mentioned at the time that a dog was sometimes provided as company for a horse. The young woman was in due course the recipient of a suitable decoration. There seems to be a recollection that the dog's kennel was subsequently washed ashore in the Dunstaffnage area. The masts of the sunken ship were visible for many years.

John Burrows was engaged in transporting Welsh coal for bunkering steam yachts, and he realised that adequate storage was essential. Accordingly, he acquired two large sailing-ship hulks, which he moored off his yard at Kerrera. In the early years of the present century, he had 'Mount Pleasant' built. This is a large, stone-built house at Kerrera, which is a notable landmark from Oban. This house has had several occupants, and one in particular had somewhat wide ramifications, rather doubtful and illegal!

The late John McDonald was a well-known builder of small craft at his yard, round from the Railway Pier, and he apparently knew of some of the activities of John Burrows.

There was an occasion when Lord - - - - was desirous of having his steam yacht surveyed on the slip at Galanach in the Sound of Kerrera. (Galanach, which is three miles south of Oban, is a Gaelic name—'Field of the Standing Stones'—and is the site of the U.K. terminal of the G.P.O.'s Atlantic Cable). The craft duly arrived, but her Captain expressed doubts as to whether the slipway was sufficiently strong to accommodate his ship. The answer was spontaneous. There was a hill behind the slipway, and it was conveyed to the Captain that, 'If your lord wants the yacht put up on the hill, there, it can be done!'

According to a local informant, the following incident took place. On one occasion it was found necessary to proceed to Upper Loch Etive to arrange for yacht moorings. The steam tender was used and, along with two of his men, John Burrows proceeded under the Connel Bridge to the desired location. As they arrived at the particular spot, they were viewed with disfavour by two Bailiffs. However, with salmon nets in the near vicinity, this was not surprising! In due course the Bailiffs thawed because of their participation in a generous provision of whisky. Their apparent opposition gradually receded to the extent where they were no longer obstacles to the carrying out of the mission— indeed they had become incapable! This happened on a Saturday afternoon and, with the tide favourable, and their work completed, they proceeded down Loch Etive, with the addition of a number of salmon which had become detached from their nets! Now, John Burrows could be a hospitable fellow, and on the way down Loch Etive, he had offered his two helpers some whisky which was left, and which they promptly liquidated. As their intoxication became absolute, the tender arrived on Sunday morning at the North Pier, Oban, which was quite near the Church where the two men were Elders. They were carried in turn to the Esplanade, where they were deposited in an incapable state.

John McDonald also related that a town council steam roller of considerable size and weight had crashed out of control through the Esplanade railings and landed on the beach. The Council duly invited various firms to tender for its re-establishment, roadwise. It did transpire that the offer of John Burrows was considered to be very low, and he was awarded the work, not without consternation among the other contractors. Now, to say the least, John Burrows was resourceful, and in due course a flat-bottomed barge was placed in position at a suitable state of the tide and close to the Esplanade. Next, a set of suitable 'sheer-legs' was assembled on the barge and with suitable lifting tackle, and the barge grounded. The road roller was returned to the road in one lift. Other tenderers had made provision for dismantling and re-assembling at a much greater price.

The author remembers John Burrows coming alongside the *Sterlina* with the water-tender to fill up the tank. The wee boy was handed the delivery hose, but curiosity asserted itself at the delay. A look at the pipe happened to coincide with the starting of the pump, and the jet of water was misdirected, to the laughter of John Burrows.

THE CONNEL BRIDGE

THIS bridge, over the Falls of Lora, can be navigated only according to tidal condition. On a motoring journey south, the writer observed a coaster proceeding to Bonawe Granite Quarry, which was seen to defy the tidal conditions and, as it approached, it was repeatedly swept backwards by the strong tide— an instance of careless navigation with the possibility of shipwreck.

Incidentally, the charge for a car over the Connel Bridge was ten shillings, which, in those days, was considered exorbitant, but, after a great deal of opposition, the charge was subsequently reduced, and ultimately waived.

⚓   ⚓   ⚓   ⚓   ⚓

JAMES BURROWS

JAMES BURROWS had a Puffer, the *Rachel*, a trim craft and always maintained in A1 condition, with a graceful and distinctive mast. The mast was always a distinctive feature and lent character, to the extent that one could easily identify a Puffer by it.

The *Rachel* was not a big carrier and therefore, a limited profit maker, and it was not surprising that the thoughts of James turned to something larger. It so happened that a shipbuilding yard had been established in Larne, Northern Ireland, and in due course, the *Petrel* was ordered and completed there in 1897.

This new craft was somewhat revolutionary. It had a well-fitted cabin aft with a good bunk capacity. The approximate measurements were as follows: length 66 ft., breadth 18 ft., hold depth 8½ ft., maximum load 129 tons.

Here again the *Petrel* carried a distinctive mast, so rigged that her big mainsail could be utilised when conditions were favourable. The craft was employed in the coastal trade for quite a number of years. The usual practice was to carry a cargo of domestic coal outwards from the General Terminus (the destination could have been Mull, Skye and the Outer Hebrides), and if possible to obtain an inwards cargo of sand, granite or timber. Quite often these Puffers would carry a grab and a suitable riddle or screen, and the inclusion of these articles made it possible to load by the crew at Loch Sunart or other locations. (The riddle ensured that only sand was deposited in the hold.)

Another lucrative trade was coal to Northern Ireland, and a return cargo of limestone from Carnlough or Glenarm. Both of these commodities were in regular production in Northern Ireland (where, of course, there was little or no coal); and in Glasgow at the Custom House Quay, where limestone and granite were discharged, it was necessary to lower the mast to sail under the Jamaica Bridge. The mast was located in a box arrangement called the 'tabernacle'.

The *Petrel*, along with similar vessels, was on service at Scapa Flow in the Orkneys, and the work done was a valuable contribution to the conduct of the war in that quarter. The Captain and Owner had his home in Glasgow, and on one occasion, a telegram arrived in the night hours. When the messenger delivered the envelope, no one in the household had courage enough to open it. The reason for the hesitation was that one of James Burrows' daughters had a young man who was on service in an active war sector. Could this be an ominous message of dread tidings? At last, with trembling hands the envelope was opened and the message was—'Send one ham!'

On one occasion the *Petrel* was outward-bound and a meal had just been partaken. Lachie, the deck hand, had appeared from the fo'c'sle with the used dishes. He was in the act of washing them when the Captain growled out, 'Lachie, throw these dishes over the side.' Lachie was in an accommodating frame of mind and just did what he was told. Jam jars had to be substituted for mugs. Lachie had been judged to be taking too long for the washing-up operation.

In the days of the steam-propelled Puffer, the cleaning of the boiler fire was an extremely hot job. It was usually done in two halves. The one was removed with a long-handled 'clot' to the engine-room floor (metal). On the now bare bars a nucleus of coal was transferred from the top of the other half, and a light dressing of coal was deposited on top. When this became alight, further fuel was added, and when at a satisfactory stage, the operation was repeated on the other half. The firing of the boiler (usually the upright type) could, in stormy weather, be an arduous task, where correct balance was essential. When the boat pitched over in one direction, the boiler shovel was filled at the bunker access and, with the loaded shovel, one waited for the return roll to empty the shovel. Such experience does not now arise with the advent of the internal combustion engine. Incidentally, the space saved by the somewhat large and weighty upright boiler must have been considerable, and it would be assumed that the carrying capacity of the vessel would be increased to some extent.

The *Petrel* was maintained in excellent condition, but with the death of James Burrows in the 1930s, a deterioration became obvious. For instance, it was not long before the lovely mast came in for decapitation, and the vessel ran for quite a time in such a condition. Latterly she was used mostly for sand, which was loaded in the Cardross region, and it was at Cardross that she had a boiler explosion and became a total wreck.

It should be stated in conclusion that the *Petrel* was fast moving as her type went, and this led to quite a few speed contests. There was one occasion when a sheriff officer had to go from Oban to evict the occupants of a house on one of the nearby islands. This was distasteful to James Burrows, however, as the *Petrel* had steam up, the voyage commenced. The official was standing astern, and by some unfortunate circumstance, clouds of steam vapour started to emerge from the engine-room casing, making it look like an inferno. The boiler gauge glass had come into contact with somebody's boot and was smashed.

Doctor McKelvie was quite a personality in Oban, and it was not unknown for him to go to an urgent case by Puffer. He made no distinction, and on one occasion he made the trip by this means of transport to attend a tinker woman.

He was a very human person, and the story is told of a woman in Oban who continually pestered him with her somewhat imaginary ailments. On this particular occasion, his 'shadow' stopped him outside the railway station with her complaints. 'I'm nearly deid, Doctor,' she said. He looked at her and ordered her to open her mouth wide with her eyes shut tight. This she obviously regarded as important, for she was left on the footpath while the Doctor moved silently away in the direction of the south-bound train, which he no doubt joined with a sigh of relief and certainly a chuckle to himself! There is a hospital in Oban bearing the name of McKelvie.

OTHER PUFFERS—THE HAMILTON SAGA

THE name of Hamilton is synonymous with the Puffer trade, and the perseverance of the Hamilton family is something to call for the deepest admiration and respect. It had its beginning with the building of the timber-framed boat, the *Glencloy*.

In 1895, Adam Hamilton, together with his sons George and Gavin, set themselves the task of building the first *Glencloy*. The site for building was in the area of the Cloy river, near Brodick. The three Hamiltons did not work trade union hours, but theirs was the satisfaction of seeing the development of a new ship without the use of modern tools.

We read that the *Glencloy* had to be taken to Glasgow to have her machinery installed at the Kingston Dock. This was a towing job, and the Hamiltons' resourcefulness was again in evidence, when it was decided to load the ship with sand where that commodity could command a ready sale in Glasgow. It was planned that the freight from the sand cargo would defray the cost of towage.

At that particular date a new era in ship construction was approaching. The iron ship had been in common use for many years, from 1818, when the *Vulcan* was built at the Monkland Canal. The Hamilton family were certainly aware of the potentiality of the general and in particular, the West Highland cargo trade, and so, in 1904, the first *Invercloy* was added, followed in 1910 by the *Rivercloy*, both products of Larne. These were followed in due course by the second *Glencloy* and second *Invercloy*, both built by Scott & Sons, Bowling, in 1930 and 1934 respectively. Eventually George Hamilton was in charge of the *Rivercloy* and his brother Gavin took over the *Invercloy*.

The Hamiltons' one aim was to make money, and it was a tribute to them that people in the Puffer trade suggested that they had enough gold to fill the hold of one of the *Cloys*. To make a success of such a venture called for some sort of office, where enquiries for cargoes could be dealt with, an essential link and one in which many Puffer owners fell short. Then there was the need not to be too choosey in relation to cargoes and their locations. The *Cloys* were run by four of a crew and, given reasonably good weather, the boats were driven on without delay. A great deal of sand was uplifted at Loch Sunart in the Sound of Mull, and it was successfully handled by a mechanical 'grab' and riddling screens. There could also be a cargo of timber for Glasgow, which could be rafted out to the Puffer and loaded by the steam winch. Another cargo source was from the granite quarries at Upper Loch Fyne. The one overriding factor was that it did not pay to have a Puffer running without a cargo on board.

MORE ABOUT THE 'PETREL'

THE *Petrel* usually had a crew of four. The Skipper and Owner, James Burrows, Willie Sutherland who came from Thurso, and two other deckhands. Willie was second in command. James Burrows was then in his seventies.

The usual routine was to make the Kyles of Bute on a Saturday evening—and drop anchor there overnight—not a popular decision with the remaining crew members. One can imagine the cold and wet anchor chain on a dark morning, with a candle enclosed in a glass globe for light, and one or two turns on the winch drum, finally attached to the davit and hauled aboard. Willie knew how to handle the situation, but usually had perforce to listen to an order from the bridge, to which he would answer an abrupt 'Shut up!' That was one form of address that the Skipper resented and there wouldn't be much, if any, conversation until Ardrishaig and the Crinan Canal was reached. Gradually relations would become normal on board. (The alternative route would, of course, have been to have made fast at Ardrishaig Pier.)

Incidentally, the anchorage in the Kyles of Bute was near where some of the dead Norwegians of the Battle of Largs were buried—rather a strange burial place and far removed from the battlefield. The anchorage was known as the Black Farlane.

On that voyage to Campbeltown and on making for Ardlamont Point, the *Petrel* came across a large cargo liner which James Burrows rather hastily informed, 'You can't go through that way.' There was no relative answer except that a fairly large coaster appeared, and it had obviously been awaiting the arrival of the larger ship which was overloaded, according to the Plimsoll marks. The buoyancy of the sea-water is greater than that up river. A fine could have been a possible outcome.

The Skipper pointed out a unique estate on the approach to the Kyles of Bute. It was owned by Campbell of South Hall, who had taken part in the Battle of Waterloo, and actually had trees planted to represent the location of the French army. During the last war, Commandos had played havoc with the house and forest.

Not far from this spot lived George Matheson, famous for his hymn compositions—'O Love that wilt not let me go' and 'Make me a captive, Lord.' George Matheson became blind at an early age, but it is a fact that the first hymn mentioned was inspired and written in a matter of minutes. Such was his faith and his closeness to his God.

With reference to cargo handlers or stevedores, at that time, there were two families involved. The MacMillans were recognised as the premier concern, but there entered another group which increased the competition.

The *Petrel* had anchored in Loch Ranza on the Saturday afternoon in rather stormy weather, in the Sound of Kilbrannan, but this did not deter the other crowd of cargo handlers from making the rough-weather passage from Campbeltown to Loch Ranza. They tied their fishing skiff to the *Petrel* and remained on board until the arrival at Campbeltown on Sunday evening. As it is often said, 'Possession is nine points of the law,' and they were safely established on the *Petrel*, ready to unload the coal cargo. Their persistence had to be admired.

The three Burrows brothers, while young men, transferred their activities from the Lagan area, near Belfast, to the west coast of Scotland. John, the eldest, became established in a ship-repairing business with a slipway at the yard on the Island of Kerrera, and also a slipway at Galanach in the Sound of Kerrera. There was an extensive trade with the many steam yachts which continually arrived at Oban. There was a big coaling business, and Welsh coal was predominantly in demand. John Burrows was on the spot to supply this coal. The amazing thing was that these three men frequently played practical jokes which reasonably could have endangered human life, but strangely, never did.

The youngest of the three brothers, Richard, was engaged in the Puffer trade. Perhaps it could be observed that he was the least affluent of the three. Fortune did not smile on him. He was, however, a very efficient navigator, and had a good knowledge of the intricate West Coast. At a comparatively early age, he was Master of the Puffer *Bruce*, which was built at Kelvindock, Maryhill. The *Bruce* was a good, well-built boat, but on one occasion she had just left Irvine, when the cargo shifted and she capsized. Richard Burrows was found clinging to a piece of wreckage some five hours after the foundering, and was apparently dead. In fact, his rescuers had come to that conclusion when the Skipper of a tug appeared and forced some whisky between his lips. The tug Skipper was a friend of Richard's, and a slight flicker was observed.

By the end of last century, Richard had acquired the *Sterlina*, another Maryhill product. Smaller than the average craft of her kind, she had a carrying capacity of about 75 tons. The single-cylinder engine made the boat a real Puffer. In common with other Maryhill craft, the *Sterlina* carried a big mainsail, and this was widely used. She was of a narrower beam than most, and could sail like a yacht: she was very suitable for carrying slates from the Ballachulish and other quarries. There exists an enlarged photograph of the *Sterlina* loading slates at Ballachulish, the quality of slate from which quarry was rated very high in the building industry.

As boys, Richard's two sons made quite a few journeys on the *Sterlina*, and a sight not to be forgotten was of David MacBrayne's *Columba* and *Iona* crossing each other's paths at high speed. They presented such a picture with their decorative scheme of red, black and gold—and what a turn of speed! The *Columba* was the more popular of the two, but certain knowledgeable seafarers had a conviction that the *Iona* had it for speed. Their cutter bows were a feature.

Richard Burrows appeared to be gifted with a measure of 'second sight'— on several occasions, during the hours of sleep, he was aware of the death of a relative in the Belfast area. There was one occasion when Richard was sitting quietly on a Sunday afternoon on the hatch of his Puffer at Port Glasgow. He was in company with other crewmen, and the conversation was naturally about the sea and boats. It happened to be a pleasant afternoon and things generally were quiet. Richard suddenly remarked that a cargo vessel which was ready for launching was moving down the 'ways' and in Richard's words, 'She launched herself and came to rest on a sandbank.' Richard was not given to undue exaggeration and it would be interesting to know if a ship did, in fact, launch herself.

Several boat-building yards were located on the Forth and Clyde Canal in addition to the Maryhill Yard, owned and managed by the McNicoll family. There was the Hamilton Hill yard owned by Burrell & Co., whose total production was in excess of 60 Puffers. Then there was a great deal of activity at Kirkintilloch where P. McGregor & Co. and J. & J. Hay were active. This eventually resolved itself into the production by Messrs. McGregor of a group of coasters with internal combustion engines. Larger craft emerged, and some of these made the initial trip to the Clyde, carrying a section which was fitted or joined on to the vessel proper. All had names with the prefix 'Innis', such as *Innisdhu*.

Those designed to use the Crinan Canal could have a length of about 84 ft. In recent years even larger coasters of the Puffer type have been built, such as *Glenfyne*, the third *Glencloy*, etc.

PUFFERS AND THEIR OWNERS

THERE were some companies which had a good participation in the West Highland trade. One such firm in the early 1900s was Paton & Hendry, and they had quite a large fleet of Puffers. A few of these could almost always be seen on the Canal stretch above the Maryhill Locks. These boats were often in for engine or boiler repairs, and there was a Superintendent Engineer in charge. As far as boiler repairs were concerned, the 'Super' had been given the advice that the sealing mixture would be more effective if beer was used instead of water. This course was decided on, and it must be left to the imagination to decide how much beer was consumed and how much was used as a mixing agent. A number of these Puffers were built by Scott & Sons Bowling.

D

Another group of Puffers which reached large dimensions was that of J. & J. Hay, the majority being built in their yard at Kirkintilloch, with names such as *Druid*, *Cossack* and *Kaffir*. As already mentioned, the other shipyard at Kirkintilloch, that of P. McGregor & Co., built the *Innis* group, propelled by internal combustion engines (presumably paraffin), which at that time— First World War period—had no great degree of reliability.

The lighthouse ship *Hesperus*, based at Oban, had continually to be bunkered by a Puffer, which carried the coal from Glasgow terminus. It was a laborious and dirty job unloading the coal to such a spic-and-span yacht-like ship as the *Hesperus*.

The evolution of the oil-fired boiler and the eventual installation of the internal combustion engine marked a great advance in maritime propulsion and cleanliness.

There was one outstanding Puffer, the *Warlight* by name, which must have been the fastest of her time. She always seemed to have plenty of steam pressure and it was stated that instead of the upright type, she had one of the marine type boilers. The *Warlight* could just negotiate the Crinan Canal, and her length was about 86 ft. This craft was, however, of the old era, where crews' accommodation was of a rather mundane order. The accommodation was accepted as such and nobody seemed unduly worried about it. As time passed, a more modern vessel appeared, as a result of the revolutionary process which had taken place. The early Puffer, for instance, had all its accommodation for the Skipper and crew in the fo'c'stle. There was no cabin aft. The machinery had also reached the stage where a compound engine operated in conjunction with a surface condenser. The Kelvindock Company kept adequately in pace with this progress, and by the end of 1900, a vessel had made its appearance complete with a stern cabin and the machinery improvements already referred to.

The earlier vessels made use of a mainsail, while others were equipped with a 'leg of mutton'-type sail. The mainsail included a gaff, and the derrick was used as a boom, the falls of which were located on the engine-room casing, forward end. The 'leg of mutton' sail, triangular in shape, did not have attachment to the derrick. The *Petrel* carried a large mainsail, and it is remembered that, on one occasion, after a night at anchor in the Kyles of Bute, she made the run to Campbeltown with a cargo of barley in record time. The wind was a fair one, off the Skipness coast, and the sail became the main source of motive power. The sight was viewed with admiration by the Campbeltown stevedores as the *Petrel* proceeded on her way.

There were two Puffers built at Dumbarton, but their construction was such that they 'loaded by the heid' with the stern up. Even with a cargo of coal they were 'doon at the heid'. About the only cargo where they appeared in proper trim was granite or sand. It was without doubt a type of craft which called for specialisation in design.

The two Puffers, *Elizabeth* and *Craigielea*, had colouring of their funnels resembling that of the *Lord of the Isles*. The *Elizabeth* was built at Port Glasgow in 1866 for Donald Whyte, but was managed by George Halliday of Rothesay.

Most of the Clyde Puffer fleets have become amalgamated—those of Colin Macphail, G. & G. Hamilton and J. & J. Hay, as Hay, Hamilton Ltd., later itself combined with Ross & Marshall's 'Light' Shipping Co., Ltd. to form Glenlight Shipping Ltd., now a subsidiary of Clyde Shipping Co., Ltd.

One Puffer, the *Victor* (of J. & J. Hay), seemed to be attached to the Clyde Trust for supplying coal for dredging activities. She was usually covered in 'glaur' but the little *Victor* seemed to devote herself to her menial task, very necessary river work. Incidentally, dredging was an important factor in the maintenance of Clyde Navigation, and there was a constant movement of 'Hoppers' with mud to a point near the Garroch Heads. These old-time hoppers had very long funnels, although that did not detract from the appearance of the craft. The length of the funnel was to encourage draught for the boiler fires. However, it has been noticed that the later additions (oil-fired) have much shorter funnels where, no doubt, forced draught is applied by a fan. These hoppers had a similar run to the *Shieldhall* and *Dalmarnock*, the two Glasgow Corporation sewage sludge ships. Like the Hoppers, they used to have long funnels, but on conversion to oil burning, had them considerably shortened; and the new ships in service are very pleasing to the eye. It was a practice of the Glasgow Corporation to issue permits to groups of members of the public to participate in voyages 'doon the watter', and it should be stated that the passenger accommodation was of a very high order; this practice has been continued by Strathclyde Regional Council with the *Garroch Head,* on which the accommodation is even better.

THE VIC PUFFERS

THE building of these vessels in England, at various ports (and two at Kirkintilloch). provided two useful and utility types of vessel. Quite a few were built during the Second World War, and were equipped with a fast-moving power unit. Two of the smaller Vic boats were taken over by Ross & Marshall; and one was seen at Crinan Basin, her Skipper being Willie Sutherland. Several of these and of the larger prefabricated type, found their way into established Puffer fleets.

⚓   ⚓   ⚓   ⚓   ⚓

BALLACHULISH

REFERENCE has been made to the *Sterlina*, and it is worth recalling that this vessel was on one occasion engaged in the loading of slates at the Ballachulish jetty, which was only sufficient in capacity to take one Puffer. The work of loading was suspended for a while because it became known that there was to be the funeral of one of the oldest inhabitants. The cortege duly arrived at the jetty, and it was found necessary to carry the coffin over the *Sterlina* to a launch which had pulled alongside. Then there was a pause when it was made known that the deceased's younger brother had still to arrive. He was eventually in attendance and his appearance suggested that he must have been not far short of a hundred years of age. When the funeral party were all aboard the launch, it was decided to proceed to the burial place—a small island not far from the jetty, possibly a quarter to half a mile. It was known as St. Mungo's Island, and it was the recognised place of interment for the Macdonald clan. It was barren and overgrown and was inhabited by a number of sheep. The Island was regarded as being sacred, and strangers were not encouraged to go there.

The village of Ballachulish was not far from the jetty, and it used to be said that the population was badly affected by 'rickets', a bone complaint of which the chief cause was lack of sunshine, because the village was overshadowed by mountains, including those of Glencoe. The district is one of the most beautiful in Scotland.

The writer can recall falling into the hold of the *Sterlina* at the slate quarry— in the act of rising, he missed catching hold of the coaming and landed over 5 ft. down, luckily breaking no bones.

⚓   ⚓   ⚓   ⚓   ⚓

THE RAISED BEACHES OF JURA

ON one occasion when the Puffer was proceeding along the Sound of Jura, the existence of these beaches was pointed out. They extend for several miles, and the extraordinary feature is that they are some 50 ft. above the present high-water mark. Their existence could be described as a phenomenon, because there are shells and shingle as on ordinary beaches, which would suggest that at one time the sea must have covered them—a most extraordinary state of affairs.

BY THE WAY

FEW people are aware that there was, in the late 1700s, a craft or a hulk anchored at the mouth of the River Cart at its junction with the River Clyde. (A hulk was usually a former sailing-ship bereft of masts and sails.) In this case it became known as the 'Floating Pub', owned and managed by Thomas Orr, known as Tam, who was born at Paisley in the year 1746 and actually died there on 25th September, 1834 from cholera at the age of 88. Tam owned fishing and other vessels which operated in the area of the junction of the rivers Cart and Clyde and these vessels had the 'Floating Pub' as their head-quarters. It is on record, or handed down, that this was a place where arrangements could be made, including— (1) The smuggling of brandy and tobacco dropped overside in the Firth of Clyde and picked up by associates. Thomas Orr's eldest son John was a fisherman at Largs. Pick-up locations were said to be Inverkip and the Cumbrae; (2) Crew-recruiting centre for deep-sea vessels from Glasgow, outward bound.

Tam and his wife, who had 12 children, were interred either in Paisley Abbey or in the Abbey Yard. The informant avers that 'He was neither hung nor had his throat cut.'

GOUROCK AND ITS BAY

WHAT an interesting and romantic place is Gourock, with its town, its bay and its pier.

Perhaps the greatest memory is the competition by the Clyde Passenger Steamers of the early 1900s to 'Get there First!' The area outside Gourock was certainly not regarded as a smokeless zone, and let it be understood that practically all these passenger boats were coal burners. So much for that, a memory remains of greetin' and happy youngsters and the Glesca vernacular.

The Bay was full of interest and romance, with the splendid array of steam and large sailing yachts. The Coats family alone were conspicuous at the anchorages with such stately ships as the *Gleniffer*. There were steam yachts at times under charter to mostly influential people—yachts such as the *Queen Margaret* and *Saxon*. One could stand on the pier at Gourock and almost be sure of seeing motor-boats or rowing-boats plying between the pier and the parent craft.

Gourock has for many years been a popular rendezvous for the Pilot Ships, which are continually on call. With the tendency to move towards the closure of the Glasgow Docks, the Pilots' work could be materially reduced, but perhaps compensated by an increase of shipping to the Greenock container terminal and docks.

With the closure of Craigendoran Pier to such ships as the *Waverley* and the *Maids*, there was an interesting newcomer which maintained a regular service between Gourock and Helensburgh—the *Countess of Kempock*, originally built for service on the inland Loch Awe. Her term of service began in May, 1936, and she was a product of Denny's of Dumbarton, then named *Countess of Breadalbane* and, as would be expected, the builders provided an excellent ship. Whereas the *Countess* was assembled on the Loch shore by prefabricated sections, it was not possible to put such an operation in reverse. It was in the spring of 1952 that arrangements were finalised for the removal of the *Countess* from Loch Awe to the Clyde, and her superstructure was dismantled. On Sunday, 20th April, transport arrangements were complete, and the task was undertaken by heavy-power units of Pickfords. The hull weighed almost 100 tons, and was conveyed on two bogies. One of the main problems was to manoeuvre the load from almost water level to the existing Loch Awe road, an operation which lasted several hours. The hull was almost 100 ft. long, and the route was via Dalmally and Inveraray. The road was hazardous, but patience and a speed of about 5 m.p.h. had their reward. Finally the *Countess of Breadalbane* was launched into Loch Fyne at Inveraray, in preparation for towage to the Clyde for refit. The transition costs seem to have been justified, for she became a useful member of the Clyde fleet, and has recently moved north again for a new service with Staffa Marine, thereafter in 1981 from Oban.

Another memorable craft at Gourock Bay was a Turkish warship, which it is thought, bore the name of *Gladiator*. On a summer's night at sunset, the crew could be seen assembled sternwise, engaged in their devotions, presumably to Allah. This vessel certainly added a touch of romance to the surroundings.

Gourock Bay is memorable for the shoals of mackerel which moved near the surface on a summer's night, and they could be caught easily with a very simple lure, such as a feather or a piece of tinfoil on a fly rod.

What a vantage point the pier was, where the movements of up-and down-river ships could be observed. The larger ships took the mid-channel course, but the Puffers and suchlike kept close to Gourock, and outward bound, the course was North East and South West to Toward Light, and thence through the Kyles of Bute.

The Glasgow–Gourock service had a locomotive which could usually be seen arriving at platform 12 or 13 at Glasgow Central Station. It was highly polished and must have been regarded with great pride by its crew. Named *Barochan*, it was owned by the Caledonian Railway Co. before grouping into the L.M.S. Railway and subsequent nationalisation.

It was possible around 1925–26 to leave Glasgow Central about 6 p.m. and travel by train to Gourock, where a Clyde steamer was boarded. Then followed an evening cruise on the Firth of Clyde, to perhaps Rothesay, and the return to Gourock. A train returned the passengers to Glasgow Central, arriving about 10-30 p.m. The cost of the outing was 3/3d.

⚓   ⚓   ⚓   ⚓   ⚓

AN INCREDIBLE STORY

THE MacBrayne boat had tied up for the evening after an active day's running The aroma of the occasional cigar and wine still lingered. The white table cover had been removed, and at the table sat the Captain and the Purser—on the table the day's takings. The process of separation and allocation began, and one pound note would be put in front of the Captain—likewise one pound note in front of the Purser. The incredible story goes on until we reach the point where a pile of change stood in isolation on the table. The question of its disposal was raised, but it was agreed to let Davie have it because he owned the boat!

This incredible story was in circulation around the 1920s, and who was the instigator was never known. It probably had no relation to fact, and was idle gossip.

Incidentally, there was an interesting story of the First Officer on one of David MacBrayne's West Highland boats. Many passengers had embarked at a certain pier, and the deck contained a great deal of luggage. There was one rather fussy female passenger who kept up a regular tirade of questions to the First Mate. At first his manner was reasonably accommodating, but as time passed, his patience became strained almost to breaking point. Finally he became rather enraged and told this passenger, 'Oh, go to Hell!' Now this was regarded as highly irregular by the passenger, so she sought out the Captain with her complaint. The harassed Mate was still in the toils, when approached by his Captain and the passenger. 'This lady complains of your rudeness, and that you told her to 'Go to Hell!' In his Highland accent the poor fellow remarked, 'Dear, dear, did I say that to you?' 'Yes, you did,' answered the complainant, 'and I am very much annoyed.' 'I told you to go to Hell?' 'Yes, you did.' 'Well, its all right now, you needn't bother to go there now.'

Some of the MacBrayne's sailors took a certain degree of pride in recalling ships they sailed on, and in later, retiral years, stories were often exchanged under the 'Heilandman's Umbrella', in Argyle Street, Glasgow. One sailor had handled, with a certain measure of pride and efficiency, the operation of the bow rope on the *Iona*. The throwing of the heaving line could be a feat in itself as its coils unfolded, and the distance covered could be considerable. An accomplished operator could usually establish contact with the pier, without many misses. The end of the heaving line was attached to the hawser, which in turn was controlled by a capstan. Donald remarked with a great deal of pride that 'He was for two years bow rope and a half on the *Iona.'*

Then there was the native of Port Askaig in Islay. When the Puffer *Sylph* arrived, he said, 'Gosh, no name!' He had always seen the name on the paddle-box of the MacBrayne boats, but *Sylph*, being screw-propelled, had none but had the name on the bow and stern.

THE CLYDE 'CLUTHAS'

WE read that in April, 1884, the Clyde Trust began a service of small passenger steamers on the Clyde for the convenience of workers and other people who were employed in shipyards and works near the River. These small ships were named 'Clutha', and were numbered as against having individual names. They were quite fast, having adequate power and propelling machinery.

The service was maintained between the Stockwell Bridge and Whiteinch, with adequate calls *en route*. The fare was one penny for one or more stages. Around 1903, these smart little ships were laid up, chiefly because of the progress of other forms of transport, particularly the electric tramcars. The

Clyde Trust retained two 'Cluthas', one as a general service unit and one as a yacht, but the remaining members of the fleet were sold off to various concerns on the East and West coasts.

⚓   ⚓   ⚓   ⚓   ⚓

'BARON VERNON' AND 'METAGAMA'

THE *Baron Vernon* was a Hugh Hogarth cargo ship, and the *Metagama* was a Canadian Pacific passenger liner, familiarly known as the 'Bride' ship. On this particular occasion, both ships were abreast of the River Leven at Dumbarton, when the *Baron Vernon* was struck on the broadside and sunk. The channel is not particularly broad at that point, but there was a theory among certain Puffer men that a contributory cause of the collision was a strong 'fresh' coming from the Leven and of sufficient force to swing the *Baron Vernon* off her straight course. In due course, the *Baron Vernon* was raised and taken to the Govan drydock. The *Metagama* was not very seriously damaged. (She was called the 'Bride' ship on account of the many young couples making their way to Canada to settle down there.)

Incidentally, boats of the Puffer type had to exercise great care in the navigation of the narrow channel of the Clyde, with an overtaking large draught ship. The suction could be so great that the smaller craft could be drawn in with considerable impact, and resultant damage, almost to the point of sinking.

⚓   ⚓   ⚓   ⚓   ⚓

UPPER LOCH FYNE

JUST south of Inveraray there are situated two granite quarries, and these could provide an inwards cargo to Glasgow. The quarries, which still operate, are at Crarae and Furnace, and both were involved in blasting misadventures. The more serious accident occurred at Crarae Quarry on the 25th September, 1886, when the Clyde river steamer, *Lord of the Isles*, carried a party from Glasgow. These included the Lord Provost of Glasgow, the Provosts of Govan and Kinning Park and various officials, all interested in the supply of granite for roadmaking. Altogether the ship carried some thousand people to Crarae.

Preparatory borings extended some 60 ft. inwards from the rock face, with branch chambers at intervals of 20 ft. to the left and right of the central chamber. At a given cannon signal from the *Lord of the Isles*, the explosion took place and thousands of tons of granite were dislodged. A number of passengers from the pleasure steamer proceeded ashore to the quarry entrance. Almost immediately there was chaos and confusion. First a dog collapsed, then a child, and various other people were in a state of collapse. Six people died and almost 30 others were seriously affected. The cause was an accumulation of noxious gases almost at ground level.

The quarries at Crarae and Furnace have continued to supply cargoes of setts for road making, granite chips and dust, and a boat of the Puffer type can be quickly loaded to the extent of 125 tons, at the quarries. The demand for setts has lessened, owing to the precedence of other forms of road making.

There was a Puffer, *Ormsa*, built at Larne, and on one occasion she was loaded with granite at one of the quarries. She then had been renamed *Moonlight* by her new owners. The voyage had been begun at the quarries and the *Moonlight* was in the vicinity of Ardlamont Point, where the weather can be very treacherous. Suddenly a wave or waves engulfed the boat, which immediately capsized with the loss of the crew. There was speculation at the time as to whether she had been properly hatched with tarpaulins and wedges.

In due course, a new and larger *Moonlight* appeared, but a few years ago she met with much the same fate, and capsized off the Isle of Man with a regretable loss of life.

The Larne-built Puffer *Petrel* was alongside the similar vessel *Logan*. The young engineer explained just how inconvenient the vessel was at close quarters. Whereas this type of ship has its engines controlled from the bridge, the particular craft was operated by some form of signalling from above. There was what is known as a 'bell-crank' lever, the object of which was to determine whether the motion was ahead or astern. The engineman was asked to move the direction of the lever from above, and it was then observed that the lever moved on the 'fulcrum pin', which had the *key missing*. A key was made in a few minutes from a square iron nail, to the appreciation of the engineman.

The point is that the vessel was negotiating the Crinan Canal without anyone being aware of this condition. The lever just didn't work.

The bell-crank lever was long enough to be within easy reach of the helmsman and of the valve control, which determined the speed of the ship. The lever can be seen on a photograph of the *Petrel*.

One of the most interesting assignments was a cargo of solid fuel for the aluminium complex at Foyers on Loch Ness. The recollection seems to be that the cargo was anthracite and it was obviously used in the manufacturing process. The 120 tons was loaded at Glasgow's Queens Dock, which is now obsolete.

The loading procedure was normal and the route was by the Crinan and Caledonian Canals. As *Petrel* approached Fort William, one became aware of the persistent sounding of the whistle, until it was realised that several East Coast steam Puffers were making for the lock at Corpach. This was to make the Canal authorities aware of the Puffers' approach, and on arrival at Corpach it was evident that a drifter had been held back to permit of the vessels making the passage together. Now the drifter being a much faster vessel, a tow rope was passed and made fast to *Petrel*, and so both vessels proceeded together by way of Loch Lochy and Loch Oich, until Fort Augustus was reached. Obviously the fuel saving on *Petrel* was considerable, and several nice fish were passed over from the towing vessel. It is interesting to know that Loch Oich was known as 'Loch Sticks' by the seafaring community, no doubt by the presence of numerous ports along its way.

A few more miles along Loch Ness and the Journey was complete, and all this happened before there was 'Monster' talk.

⚓   ⚓   ⚓   ⚓   ⚓

RIGHT OF WAY

IT is an interesting point to reflect on, that around 100 years ago there was a public right of way from Govan to Renfrew, where people could walk past the various shipyards and observe the ships in various stages of construction.

It was of wooden construction, and was such that it had to be dismantled preparatory to the launching of a ship in the particular area. It was used by horses which towed barges between Port Glasgow and Glasgow. At Renfrew, it was quite a vantage point from which to observe River traffic passing to and fro. The viewing of the engines of the old 'Clyde' at Renfrew was always interesting, and still is.

It is often remarked just how easy it is to recall childhood events as against recent happenings. How true this is! A Sunday visit to the docks along Govan Road towards the Princes Dock showed the terminal point for the Allan Line, with distinctive funnels; and the 'Boiled Egg' formation of the *Grampian* and other ships of the fleet. The Allan Line was absorbed by the Canadian Pacific Company, and contained several large ships, some double-funnelled, notably *Alsatian* and *Calgarian*. One of the C.P.R. ships built after the merger was the *Montcalm*, which, at times, engaged in short cruises in the Mediterranean Sea.

⚓　　　⚓　　　⚓　　　⚓　　　⚓

A RIVER PLATE VOYAGE

Back in 1923 the author was appointed as Fourth Engineer on the ex-Burrell ship *Strathfillan*. The point of embarkation was Ellesmere Port, and the destination was the River Plate, at two locations well up the narrowing river. Incidentally, the voyage took 27 days, and although equipped with three boilers, one of these was usually out of commission through defect, with resultant speed reduction.

It was one of those voyages where there was no rain, in fact arid conditions prevailed. Condenser trouble was much in evidence, necessitating frequent stoppages to have leaking tubes attended to, the old ship having been built around 1904, and engined by David Rowan & Sons Ltd. *Strathfillan* found its way into the fleet of the Anglo American Oil Co., but the Rowan nameplate in the engine-room always reminded one of Glasgow and the Clyde. The carrying capacity was around 8000 tons.

Eventually she arrived at Montevideo and proceeded up the River Plate on what was an interesting part of the voyage. The river narrowed considerably and abounded with insect life and fine vegetation. In due course *Strathfillan* was moored at Villa Constitucion, where bulk linseed was loaded as part cargo. The next call was at San Nicolas, where hides were loaded. An interesting fact in the loading of the hides, which were flat, was the addition of a plateful of salt scattered between each. San Nicolas was not so far up river as Rosario, which was some 180 miles from the mouth. Mosquitoes were in abundance, and their bites showed up plainly. Turtles also abounded in the river.

Then the return to Buenos Aires commenced, and that port was reached on 1st April, 1923. This was to be a never-to-be-forgotten date, for Yours Truly lost the half of his right index finger, after which followed several days and nights of near agony. There was, of course, no surgeon on board, and the treatment for the remaining stump was to be covered with a yellow powder called 'Iodoform', after which the bandage was applied and occasionally renewed. The author remembers the effeminate type of Chief Engineer producing a book of Kipling's works for myself to read, but my thoughts were elsewhere and my chief concern was—'Could I still write?' so I proceeded to my room, where I discovered that I did not use my index finger to write, but the one next to it!

Strathfillan proceeded on her way and it was hereabouts that the Chief Engineer had an attack of 'Coal Fever'. This was a condition where it was thought coal was running short, so to pacify the sleepless Chief, it was decided to anchor at Barbados and re-bunker. *Strathfillan* was invaded, or should I say, besieged by an army of native women, each carrying a basket filled with coal, and this cycle continued until the desired tonnage was reached, and the exhausted Chief regained his sleep.

So *Strathfillan* proceeded on her way northwards, until one particular night at Cape Hatteras there was a sudden drop in temperature which, it is understood, is caused by the warm waters of the Gulf Stream meeting the colder conditions of the North Atlantic Ocean. All went well, and accordingly the Brooklyn side of New York was reached, ready for unloading. Incidentally, there were seven murders during our first night at Brooklyn.

Then our thoughts turned to the homeward run, and before leaving New York, the author had a further finger operation, when the injured finger was amputated at the nearest joint. We then proceeded to Norfolk, Virginia for bunkering, and this completed, made for Baltimore (Curtis Bay) where, in 1923, there operated a coking apparatus where the wagons were of considerable size and the coke was transferred from shore to ship on something akin to a moving carpet. The *Strathfillan* was fully loaded in a few hours, and was destined for Dunkirk. The final chapter was the arrival at Cardiff, where the author arranged for his clearance and proceeded home to Glasgow.

ILLUSTRATIONS

Puffer "AILSA" — afterwards Ross & Marshall's "HEADLIGHT".

Puffer "ARDFERN" in basin at Bowling.

E

Old time puffer "ASHDALE GLEN" at Harbour, Inveraray.

Puffers "BOER" & "MELLITE" berthed at Greenock — in East India Harbour.

49

"CHINDIT" and "POLARLIGHT" (II) off Princes Pier, Greenock 31/1/59.

Coal arriving at Dunoon—the puffers "CHRYSOLITE", "BOER", "ADVANCE" and "VICTOR".

The yard of J. & J. Hay at Kirkintilloch with "CRETAN", "BOER" and "SPARTAN" (III) 1/3.58.

A Highland scene—the puffer "DANE" at Salen, Loch Sunart 31/5/50.

Two steam propelled puffers "DANE" and "SPARTAN" (III) at Bowling. 28/9/59. Lanarkshire & Dumbartonshire Railway in background.

Puffer "DANE" at Salen Loch Sunart.

54

Larger craft "DOUGLAS" off Langbank, 9/1949. Around 140 tons capacity, has been loading sand at Cardross. Observe loading grab: Owners; Warnock, Paisley.

Puffer "FAITHFUL" discharging at Highland jetty.

55

Loaded with sand—note the riddling screen—the "FAITHFUL" makes her way up the Clyde, off Newshot 31/8/50.

In a corner of Queen's Dock the "GAEL", "CUBAN" and "BOER" await their turn to load with coal.

Old time puffers at Glasgow General Terminus. "ROSIE" and "GAEL". By courtesy of Dan McDonald

The original "GLENCLOY" (I), This was the craft built on the riverside near Brodick by the Hamilton family — see 27.

Modern puffer nearest camera, "GLENCLOY" (II), berthed alongside "GLENROSA" : in the rear is a Clyde Navigation 'Hopper', used for transport of mud down River Clyde.

58

"GLENCLOY" (II) at Scalpay, Harris (funnel shortened when converted to oil-burning).

"GLENCLOY" (II) outward-bound on Clyde.

"GLENCLOY" (II) proceeding through Crinan Canal.

"GLENCLOY" (II) unloading on beach at Inverie, Loch Nevis.

60

Loaded with coal the "GREEK" prepares to leave the Canal Basin at Bowling 26/8/38.

Steam puffer "HAFTON" built at the McNicholl Bros., Kelvindock Yard at Maryhill 1910, was possibly about 100 tons loading capacity. Lost in the Firth of Lorne in 1933. (No weather protection for crew).

Steam puffer "INVERCLOY" built by Scott's of Bowling in 1934. The modernised "GLENCLOY" (II) also in picture.

Puffer "INVERCLOY" (II) built in 1934 by Scott's of Bowling, tied up in Bowling Harbour, 22/2/51.

Puffers "INVERCLOY" (II) & "GLENROSA" (I) ex "VIC 29", English built. Overhauling at Scott's Yard, Bowling, 6 1 52.

A view of Tralee Harbour, with the puffer "INVERGOWRIE" and two sailing craft.

Steam puffer "JENNIE" built at Larne in 1902 for Calum Campbell. Stranded on the island of Eigg in a fog in 1954. A splendid example of coaster construction. Photo by courtersy of Dan McDonald.

F

The steam propelled "KAFFIR" leaving Tobermory, 8/7/49.

Puffers "INCA" and "KAFFIR" at Kirkintilloch 30/3/59. "KAFFIR" steam propelled before conversion.

Remodelled "KAFFIR" during refitting, with "BOER" at Frisky Wharf, Bowling, 7/4/62.

Diesel converted puffer "KAFFIR" at Ardrishaig beside yachts, 25/8/62.

Puffer "KAFFIR" proceeding. Note conversion to Diesel with extra crew accommodation.

"KAFFIR" (Converted to Diesel) at coal pier, Dunoon, 3/7/64.

Another view of Diesel "KAFFIR", at Albert Pier, Rothesay 24/4/65.

Two converted puffers "KAFFIR" and "LASCAR" at Rothesay, 26/3/66.

Puffer "LADY MORVEN" off Gourock, 2/8/68.

"LADY ISLE" (II) (as motor vessel) leaving Rothesay, 27/1/68.

Puffer "TEXAN and "LADY ISLE" discharging coal at Dunoon. 30/12/58.

Scott's slipway at Bowling including "MAID OF ASHTON", puffer "GLENARAY" and schooner-rigged ship.

Leaving Ardrossan the "LIMELIGHT" (I) ex "VIC 23", 10.9.56.

The "LYTHE" proceeds outwards, off Langbank 5/6/39.

Scott's slipway at Bowling, with the Caledonian S.P.Co's "MAID OF ASHTON" and the puffer "GLENARAY" ex "Vic 89".

Puffers "MELLITE", "LADY ISLE" (II) and "LADY MORVEN" in East India Harbour, Greenock, 25 12 67.

Ross & Marshall puffer "MOONLIGHT" (II) ex "ORMSA" (II) proceeding down the Clyde loaded, off Old Kilpatrick in 1939. (She afterwards foundered off Ardlamont).

"MOONLIGHT" (III) with a much larger hatch and carrying capacity than "MOONLIGHT" (II).

"MOONLIGHT" (III) tying up at Portree, 21/9/60.

"MOONLIGHT" (III) at the Town Quay, Dumbarton, 20/3/61.

Stern view of "MOONLIGHT" (IV) including new apparatus for lifeboat. In Tarbert Inner Harbour 2/8/69.

"MOONLIGHT" (IV) at Greenock.

Outward bound with a following wind—the "MOOR" off Port Glasgow 1/5/39.

The Larne-built "ORMSA" (II) tied up at Drumchapel 11/7/37. Afterwards "MOONLIGHT" (II).

Puffer "NORMAN" deeply loaded outward bound.

Launch at Larne, 1897, of 'Puffer' "PETREL", carrying capacity 125 tons. Owned and skippered by James Burrows.

Puffer "PETREL" loading slates at an Argyllshire quary.

S.S. "PETREL" proceeding inward, abreast of Kilcreggan.

S.S. "PETREL" (here seen at Ardrishaig) originally owned and maintained by James Burrows. Sold to Warnock of Paisley, afterwards to McNeil of Greenock, for sand-dredging. Blown up by boiler explosion off Cardross, 19/4/51.

'Puffer' "PETREL" at Bowling. Awaiting sale after death of owner.

Puffer "PIBROCH" (I). Built by Scott & Sons, Bowling. Owned by 'White Horse' Distillers.

The second "PIBROCH" larger and of greater carrying capacity than "PIBROCH" (I). Built 1956, was chiefly engaged in carrying cargoes to and from Lagavulin Distillery in Islay. Propelled by Diesel machinery.

Loaded "PIBROCH" en route from Islay, off north end of Arran, 22/8/68.

Tendering to the Channel Fleet at Lamlash — the first "POLAR LIGHT" (I).

Puffer "RIVERCLOY" at Inveraray. Built 1910 at Larne. Owned by Hamilton Bros., Arran.

"RIVERCLOY" built at Larne 1910. A very speedy 'Puffer'. Owned by the Hamilton Brothers. Here seen in Bowling Harbour.

"ROMAN" at Old Jetty and "KILDONAN" at Pier, Brodick.

The Cloch Lighthouse near Gourock, with one of the Caledonian car ferries, "ARRAN", "BUTE" or "COWAL".

Two eras. Foreground and Arran Smack. Astern, modern puffer owned by J. Hay.

Puffer "ASHDALE GLEN" beached at Calgary Bay, Mull, with carts unloading.

Puffer "FAITHFUL". Larne-built. Carrying capacity 125 tons. Compound engined.

"GLENCLOY" (II) at Caol Ile pier unloading (Paps of Jura in background).

"GLENFYNE" at Bonahaven Distillery, Islay.

"GLENFYNE" at Corpach, Caledonian Canal.

"GLENFYNE" in Laggan Avenue, approaching Loch Oich, Caledonian Canal.

On board "GLENFYNE" : Scarba and Jura in distance.

"GLENSHIRA" (grey hull) loading coal at Ayr harbour. London & Rochester Co's. "EMINENCE" beyond.

Puffer "KAFFIR" before conversion to Diesel. Entering Crinan Canal at Ardrishaig.

Two of the English-built 'Vic' puffers, "LADY MORVEN" and "LADY ISLE" (II) at Rothesay, 21/10/72.

"SAXON" Millport-owned. Discharging coal cargo on beach. Built at Kirkintilloch by J. & J. Hay and originally owned by them.

Puffer "STARLIGHT" at Port Ellen, Islay. Skippered by W. Sutherland, owned by Ross & Marshall, Limited.

Ross & Marshall Limited's, third "STORMLIGHT", with increased crew accommodation aft. Carrying 140 tons. Here seen leaving Prince's Dock, Glasgow.

The Crinan Hotel at entrance to Crinan Canal — rebuilt after fire damage.

Puffer embroidered by 12 years old Dawn Burrows.

Model of compound engined Puffer.

Outward bound loaded Puffer abreast of Kilcreggan.

"SEALIGHT" off Greenock, outward bound 4/9/51.

H

Puffer "SMEATON" (ex "VIC 33") at Loch Aline 12/6/50.

Puffer "SMEATON" entering Crinan Canal Locks at Ardrishaig.

Proceeding up river off Langbank — the "SPARTAN" (II) ex "TIREE" 10.7.39.

"STARLIGHT" inward bound off Blythswood Light 30/5/64.

Puffer "STERLINA" at Crinan Basin: the large mainsail had been used en route and is ready for hoisting on departure. Owned and skippered by Richard Burrows who with his late eldest son is at stern.

"STERLINA" — owned and skippered by Richard Burrows. Built Maryhill 1872. First iron-built Puffer from that Yard.

"STORMLIGHT" (III) (built at Norwich in 1957).

Steam puffer "WARLOCK" at Inverness, Thornbush Harbour, which has now been filled in or reclaimed. This vessel was built at Dumbarton in 1871, of iron, with wooden bulwarks. (This part of Thornbush is not far from Beauly Firth where the New Kessock Bridge is under construction).

A puffer in the drydock: one of the 'Innis' lighters in Kelvin Dock, Maryhill.

Puffer "No. 10" unloading coal while beached at Blackwaterfoot (previously one of the Carron Company's canal boats).

ADDITIONAL OLD PHOTOGRAPHS
OF OTHER FORMS OF TRANSPORT

S.S. "BRENDA": MacBrayne-owned: Length 84 feet: Photograph by late C.L.D. Duckworth; leaving Ardrishaig Harbour in 1913 after passage through Crinan Canal. On regular service from Glasgow via the Canal to Argyllshire ports.

At Crinal R.M.S. **"CHEVALIER"**, centre **"LINNET"**. In foreground MacBrayne's **"COUNTESS OF KELLIE"**, a very unusual puffer, originally a paddle ferry boat plying between South Alloa and Alloa.

"CLAN MACNAIR" returning to Glasgow after trials.

"DALRIADA", here seen at Ayr.

An old timer, RMS "GONDOLIER" of 1866 returning to Inverness in the 1930s.

On board "DALRIADA" — very fast passenger vessel between the Clyde and Campbeltown. In Kyles of Bute, 19 6 37.

MacBrayne Paddle Steamer "GONDOLIER" at Muirtown Wharf, Inverness.

"LAIRDS ISLE" very fast and (apart from war work) was engaged in daily service from Ardrossan to Belfast. Eventually had gun mounted on stern for war service. (MacBrayne's GONDOLIER on left — at Ardrossan for refit): 2/4/36.

Canal passenger steamer "LINNET" between Crinan and Ardrishaig: also lower picture — note wearing apparel of the early 1900s.

The Crinan Canal "LINNET" owned by David MacBrayne, which carried passengers from Ardrishaig to Crinan en route for Oban.

Steamer "LINNET"

"LINNET" with passengers garbed with prevailing fashion — 1890s.

111

Miller's Bridge between Cairnbaan and Ardrishaig on the Crinan Canal. This is the point where coal was discharged for the Argyll & Bute Mental Hospital. The vessel moored at Bridge is a Gabbart while the "LINNET" is passing through.

The second "MOUNTAINEER" (originally "HERO") a popular MacBrayne ship well known in the Highlands, as also were the first and third of this name.

"QUEEN MARY" (Yard No. 534) nearing completion at Clydebank, with third funnel in course of assembly.

Clyde Shipping Co.'s "RATHLIN" — noted for war service — here seen at Cork.

"PRINCESS LOUISE". Passenger cruise ship and general carrier to and from Oban; here seen at Fort Augustus when on canal cruises from Inverness.

"SAINT COLUMBA", formerly "QUEEN ALEXANDRA", with third funnel added.

Kinlochleven Motor Vessel "SCOUT" in Oban Bay, owned by David MacBrayne Ltd. ('Mount Pleasant' can be seen under the crane jib).

Motor Vessel "SCOUT" at Kinlochleven near British Aluminium Works: just beyond, and blowing off steam, is "LOCH LEVEN QUEEN", originally "CLUTHA No. 12" (see page 38 of text).

S.S. "STRATHFILLAN" built in the early 1900s by Wm. Hamilton, Port Glasgow for the Burrell or Hungarian Steamship Company. It is presumed that ship is loading timber logs in a Swedish port. The author was fourth engineer on this ship during 1923.

Another view of Clyde Shipping Co.'s "RATHLIN".

Connel Railway Bridge spanning Loch Etive.

Group including James Burrows and eldest daughter Rachel. Reversing bell crank lever indicated by 'X'.

One of the Clyde Shipping Company's screw tugs.

Erskine Ferry with tanker proceeding upstream.

Open tramcar with driver exposed to all weathers in early 1900s. Note chain of horse drawn lorries.

A Glasgow tramcar top-covered, but again with driver exposed to all weather. About 1920.

Example of "CORONATION" type of tramcar as operated in Glasgow (along with other types) until the system was discontinued and superseded by bus services.